Folktales
ON STAGE

**Children's Plays for Reader's Theater
(or Readers Theatre), With 16 Play Scripts
From World Folk and Fairy Tales**

Aaron Shepard

Shepard Publications
Los Angeles

Author Online!

For more reader's theater, visit
Aaron Shepard's RT Page at

www.aaronshep.com/rt

ISBN-13:   978-0-938497-20-2
ISBN-10:   0-938497-20-0

Library of Congress Control Number: 2003094468
Library of Congress subject headings:
Readers' theater
Children's plays
Folklore

1.1

Contents—Short

Contents—Long

About This Book

Folktales on Stage is a collection of reader's theater scripts for young readers, adapted from my own folktale retellings. Most of the adapted stories are ones I first published as picture books or in magazines like *Cricket* or Australia's *School Magazine*. Most of the scripts themselves were first posted on my Web site in the area called Aaron Shepard's RT Page—now the Web's most popular reader's theater destination, with visits by thousands of teachers and librarians each week.

The scripts may be freely copied, shared, and performed for any educational, noncommercial purpose, except they may not be posted online without permission. Feel free to edit the scripts to serve the needs of your own readers.

A full range of reading levels is included, with the collection aimed mostly at ages 8 to 15. Recommended reading age more or less progresses through the book, from younger to older.

A primary aim of reader's theater is to promote reading. To further this, it's good to have on hand one or more copies of the book or magazine story that the script is based on.

Above all, have fun with the scripts. Let your readers discover that reading is a treat.

About the Scripts

In the "long" table of contents, and at the beginning of each script, you'll find notation on genre, culture of origin or setting, theme, number of readers, suggested reader ages, and approximate reading time, as well as a brief description of the story.

Also at the beginning of each script is a list of roles. A reader, of course, can be assigned more than one role, as long as only one role is "onstage" at a time. When a script is short on female characters, it's common to cast females in male roles.

Roles listed in parentheses are unscripted, with no assigned speech, and usually optional. These roles can be given to surplus readers if your directing style includes stage movement or if you choose to add speeches or sounds for these readers. In the reader count, unscripted roles are indicated by the phrase "or more."

These scripts are designed to be photocopied for direct use by readers. (That's why all the page numbers in the scripts are at top right!) For performing, some kind of binder will be helpful.

About Staging

Of course, an actual stage is not required for reader's theater. *Stage* here refers simply to your performance area, which could be the front of a classroom, or an open space in a one-room library, or one end of a school gym or cafeteria. (Or a script could be used as a group reading exercise, with no performance area at all.)

It's best that you first read the script—or its source story—*to* the young people. Some scripts may be challenging, and effective modeling will lead to greater benefit and enjoyment.

The readers can underline or highlight their own parts in their copies of the script, marking only words to be spoken. (Yellow non-fluorescent marker works well.) Any unfamiliar words should be looked up and checked for pronunciation and meaning. Added stage directions can go in the script margins—preferably in pencil, to allow corrections.

Your readers might also prepare an introduction to the story, for use in performance. While an introduction should always mention the title and the author, it could also discuss source, author background, cultural background, theme, or context within a longer work. But it shouldn't give away the plot! Notes at the beginning of some scripts will provide starting points. Introductions are most effective when spoken informally, rather than read or memorized exactly.

With many of the scripts, you can produce a lively stereo effect by dividing your narrators between the two ends of your stage. For instance, with four narrators, place Narrators 1 and 2 at far left, and 3 and 4 at far right, as seen from the audience. To preserve this effect with fewer readers, assign the roles of Narrators 1 and 2 to one reader, and 3 and 4 to another.

In some scripts, particular narrators may relate mostly to particular characters. Notes at the start of those scripts will suggest positioning the characters near the corresponding narrators.

There are many styles of reader's theater. In the most traditional style:

- Readers are arranged in a row or a semicircle, standing up or sitting on high stools. Typically, narrators are placed at one or both ends, and major characters in the center.
- Scripts can be held in hand or set on music stands.
- Readers look straight out toward the audience or at an angle, rather than at each other.

- Characters "exit" by turning their backs to the audience. (Narrators don't normally exit.)
- "Scene changes"—jumps in time or place—can be shown by a group "freeze," followed by some kind of collective shift.

Chamber Readers, the group with which I trained and performed for five years, employs a style quite different, designed to appeal to young audiences. (For more details, see my book *Readers on Stage*.)

- Characters portray the action described in the story. Where possible, the portrayal is literal, with characters moving around the stage much as in a play. Where necessary, it's suggestive, as with simple mime devices like walking in place.
- Though narrators look mostly at the audience, characters look mostly at each other.
- Scripts in sturdy binders are held in one hand, leaving the other hand free for acting.
- A set of low stools and perhaps one or more high stools serve as versatile stage scenery or props.
- "Exits" and "scene changes" are handled much as in traditional reader's theater.

These scripts should lend themselves to either approach, or to any other you might choose. Feel free to create your own! There *are* rules in reader's theater, but luckily there is no one to enforce them.

About the Web Site

For more resources, please visit my Web site at www.aaronshep.com. From there, click on Aaron's RT Page (www.aaronshep.com/rt) to find many more scripts, plus other help with reader's theater. Or click on "Aaron's Extras" (www.aaronshep.com/extras) for links to special features for individual scripts. These features might include printable color posters, audio recordings of names and music in the scripts, story background, and picture book info. For some scripts, you might also see a "chamber" version for smaller groups of readers.

To help you find what you need, the site includes a comprehensive search function, as well as indexes of all my stories and scripts—online and off—by title, genre, age, theme, country or region, historical period, ethnic group, religion, mythology, holiday, and activity.

And while you're visiting, be sure to sign up for my email bulletin to receive notice of new scripts and collections. There's always more to come!

The Adventures of Mouse Deer
Tales of Indonesia and Malaysia

Told by Aaron Shepard

Adapted for reader's theater by the author, from his stories appearing in Australia's *School Magazine,* Mar.–May 1997

PREVIEW: Mouse Deer is small, and many animals want to eat him—but first they have to catch him!

GENRE: Folktales, trickster tales
CULTURE: Indonesian, Malaysian
THEME: Wits vs. power
READERS: 9 or more
READER AGES: 7–10
LENGTH: 20 minutes (3 + 7 + 4 + 6 + 1)

ROLES: Narrators 1–4, Mouse Deer, Tiger, Crocodile, Farmer, Dog, (Other Crocodiles), (Scarecrow)

NOTES: For best effect, place NARRATORS 1 and 2 at far left, and 3 and 4 at far right, as seen from the audience. TIGER, FARMER, and DOG can double as OTHER CROCODILES. To increase the number of readers, a different reader can play MOUSE DEER in each story. The conversations among the NARRATORS and between them and MOUSE DEER will be more believable if the readers learn those speeches by heart and don't look at their scripts. Below is the tune for "Mouse Deer's Song," an original composition of the author's. To hear the music, and for other special features, visit www.aaronshep.com/extras.

NARRATOR 1: Today we're going to tell you three stories about Mouse Deer.

NARRATOR 2: *(to NARRATOR 1, suspiciously)* Wait a minute. Did you say "Mouse Deer"?

NARRATOR 1: That's right!

NARRATOR 4: I never heard of a "Mouse Deer"! *(to NARRATOR 3)* Did you?

NARRATOR 3: Not me! What *is* he? A mouse?

NARRATOR 1: No.

NARRATOR 2: A deer?

NARRATOR 1: No.

NARRATOR 4: *(accusingly)* Hey, are you trying to trick us?

NARRATOR 1: No! He's a real animal!

NARRATOR 3: *(skeptically)* Yeah? Then how big is he?

NARRATOR 1: About as big as a cat.

NARRATOR 2: And where does he live?

NARRATOR 1: In the jungles of Asia and Africa.

NARRATOR 4: And what does he look like?

NARRATOR 1: His legs and tail look like a deer's.

NARRATOR 2: *(starting to believe)* Well, all right.

NARRATOR 1: But his face and body look like a mouse's.

NARRATOR 3: *(accusingly again)* You're tricking us!

NARRATOR 1: It's true! That's why he's called Mouse Deer!

NARRATOR 4: *(grudgingly)* Well, *maybe* we believe you.

NARRATOR 2: Tell us some more.

NARRATOR 1: *(to other NARRATORS and audience)* Mouse Deer eats only plants, but lots of animals eat Mouse Deer. To stay alive, he has to be quick and smart. He also has to be tricky—just like Brer Rabbit and Anansi, the spider man from Africa. Mouse Deer even plays some of the same tricks.

NARRATOR 2: *(to NARRATOR 1)* You know what *I* think? I think *you're* the tricky one!

NARRATOR 4: Me too!

NARRATOR 3: That's right!

NARRATOR 1: No, I'm not! There are *lots* of stories about Mouse Deer.

NARRATOR 3: *(sarcastically)* And I bet you want us to believe they're true!

NARRATOR 1: Of course they are! *All* stories are true—even if they didn't happen.

NARRATORS 2, 3, & 4: *(confused, to audience)* Huh?

NARRATOR 1: *(to audience)* Mouse Deer has his own song too, and you can help sing it. Here's how it goes.

> I'm quick and smart as I can be.
> Try and try, but you can't catch me!

> Now *you* try it. *(helps the audience practice)*

NARRATORS 2, 3, & 4: *(join in on the practice)*

NARRATOR 1: Good! Now we're ready to go.

NARRATOR 1: In our first story, Mouse Deer meets one of his most dangerous enemies. This story is called,

MOUSE DEER: *(brightly, to audience)* Mouse Deer . . .

NARRATOR 1: and

TIGER: *(ferociously, to audience, showing claws)* . . . Tiger.

MOUSE DEER: *(to audience)* Ready to sing? *(drawing out the first note to help them join in)*
> I'm quick and smart as I can be.
> Try and try, but you can't catch me!
> *(keeps humming the tune softly to himself)*

NARRATOR 1: Mouse Deer sang his song as he walked through the forest.

NARRATOR 4: He was looking for tasty fruits and roots and shoots.

NARRATOR 2: Though he was small, he was not afraid. He knew that many big animals wanted to eat him.

NARRATOR 3: But first they had to catch him!

NARRATOR 1: Then he heard something.

TIGER: *Rowr!*

MOUSE DEER: *(gasps)*

NARRATOR 4: There was Tiger!

TIGER: *(sounding sinister)* Hello, Mouse Deer. I was just getting hungry. Now you can be my *lunch.*

NARRATOR 2: Mouse Deer didn't want to be lunch. He looked around and thought fast.

NARRATOR 3: He saw . . . a mud puddle.

MOUSE DEER: *(makes a face like he's thinking hard, then brightens, turns to TIGER)* I'm sorry, Tiger. I can't be your lunch. The King has ordered me to guard his . . . pudding.

TIGER: *(uncertainly)* His pudding?

MOUSE DEER: *(pointing)* Yes. There it is.

NARRATOR 1: Mouse Deer pointed to the mud puddle.

MOUSE DEER: It has the best taste in the world. The King doesn't want anyone else to eat it.

NARRATOR 4: Tiger looked longingly at the puddle.

TIGER: *(struggling with himself, knowing he shouldn't ask but wanting it badly)* I would like to taste the King's pudding.

MOUSE DEER: Oh, no, Tiger! The King would be very angry.

TIGER: *(pleading)* Just one little taste, Mouse Deer! The King will never know.

MOUSE DEER: Well . . . all right, Tiger. But first let me run far away, so no one will blame *me.*

TIGER: All right, Mouse Deer, you can go now.

NARRATOR 2: Mouse Deer ran quickly out of sight.

TIGER: *(delightedly, to audience)* Imagine! The King's pudding!

NARRATOR 3: He took a big mouthful.

TIGER: *(puts a handful in his mouth, freezes in surprise, then makes a horrible face and spits the mud out toward audience)* Phooey!

NARRATOR 3: He spit it out.

TIGER: Yuck! Ugh! Bleck! That's no pudding. That's *mud*!

NARRATOR 1: Tiger ran through the forest.

TIGER: *Rowr!*

NARRATOR 4: He caught up with Mouse Deer.

MOUSE DEER: *(gasps)*

TIGER: *(fuming)* Mouse Deer, you tricked me once. But now you will be my *lunch*!

NARRATOR 2: Mouse Deer looked around and thought fast.

NARRATOR 3: He saw . . . a wasp nest in a tree.

MOUSE DEER: *(thinks hard, then brightens)* I'm sorry, Tiger. I can't be your lunch. The King has ordered me to guard his . . . drum.

TIGER: His drum?

MOUSE DEER: *(pointing)* Yes. There it is.

NARRATOR 1: Mouse Deer pointed to the wasp nest.

MOUSE DEER: It has the best sound in the world. The King doesn't want anyone else to hit it.

TIGER: *(struggling with himself)* I would like to hit the King's drum.

MOUSE DEER: Oh, no, Tiger! The King would be very angry.

TIGER: Just one little hit, Mouse Deer! The King will never know.

MOUSE DEER: Well . . . all right, Tiger. But first let me run far away, so no one will blame *me.*

TIGER: All right, Mouse Deer, you can go now.

NARRATOR 4: Mouse Deer ran quickly out of sight.

TIGER: *(to audience)* Imagine! The King's drum!

NARRATOR 2: He reached up and hit it.

NARRATOR 3: *Pow.*

ALL NARRATORS: *Bzzzzzzzzzzzzz. (Each NARRATOR keeps buzzing when not speaking.)*

NARRATOR 1: The wasps all flew out. They started to sting Tiger.

TIGER: Ouch! Ooch! Eech! That's no drum. That's a *wasp nest*!

NARRATOR 4: Tiger ran away. But the wasps only followed him!

TIGER: Ouch! Ooch! Eech!

NARRATOR 2: Tiger came to a stream. He jumped in—*splash!*— and stayed underwater as long as he could.

NARRATOR 3: At last the wasps went away.

ALL NARRATORS: *(fade out with buzzing)*

NARRATOR 1: Then Tiger jumped out.

TIGER: *Rowr!*

NARRATOR 4: He ran through the forest till he found Mouse Deer.

MOUSE DEER: *(gasps)*

TIGER: *(enraged)* Mouse Deer, you tricked me once. You tricked me twice. But now you will be my *lunch*!

NARRATOR 2: Mouse Deer looked around and thought fast.

NARRATOR 3: He saw . . . a cobra! The giant snake was coiled asleep on the ground.

MOUSE DEER: *(thinks hard, then brightens)* I'm sorry, Tiger. I can't be your lunch. The King has ordered me to guard his . . . belt.

TIGER: His belt?

MOUSE DEER: *(pointing)* Yes. There it is.

NARRATOR 1: Mouse Deer pointed to the cobra.

MOUSE DEER: It's the best belt in the world. The King doesn't want anyone else to wear it.

TIGER: *(struggling with himself)* I would like to wear the King's belt.

MOUSE DEER: Oh, no Tiger! The King would be very angry.

TIGER: Just for one moment, Mouse Deer! The King will never know.

MOUSE DEER: Well . . . all right, Tiger. But first let me run far away, so no one will blame *me.*

TIGER: All right, Mouse Deer, you can go now.

NARRATOR 4: Mouse Deer ran quickly out of sight.

TIGER: *(to audience)* Imagine! The King's belt!

NARRATOR 2: He started to wrap it around himself. The cobra woke up.

NARRATOR 3: *Sssssssssssss. (keeps hissing)*

NARRATOR 1: It didn't wait for Tiger to finish wrapping.

NARRATOR 4: It wrapped itself around Tiger.

NARRATOR 2: Then it squeezed him and bit him.

NARRATOR 3: *Sstt! Sssssssssssss. (keeps hissing)*

TIGER: Ooh! Ow! Yow! That's no belt. That's a *cobra*! *(into the distance)* Help! Mouse Deer! Help!

NARRATOR 3: *(fades out with hissing)*

NARRATOR 1: But Mouse Deer was far away.

NARRATOR 4: And as he went, he sang his song.

MOUSE DEER: *(to audience)*

> I'm quick and smart as I can be.
> Try and try, but you can't catch me!

NARRATOR 1: In our second story, Mouse Deer meets another one of his most dangerous enemies. This story is called,

MOUSE DEER: *(brightly, to audience)* Mouse Deer . . .

NARRATOR 1: and

CROCODILE: *(menacingly, to audience, in low, growly voice)* . . . Crocodile.

NARRATOR 1: One day, Mouse Deer went down to the river.

NARRATOR 4: He wanted to take a drink.

NARRATOR 2: But he knew Crocodile might be waiting underwater to eat him.

NARRATOR 3: Mouse Deer had an idea. He said out loud,

MOUSE DEER: *(to himself, but loud and clear so CROCODILE hears)* I wonder if the water's warm. I'll put in my leg and find out. *(freezes till NARRATOR 1 speaks again)*

NARRATOR 4: *(to NARRATOR 1 and others)* Wait a minute! Stop the story! Mouse Deer said he'd put in his leg?

NARRATOR 2: What a dumb idea!

NARRATOR 3: I thought Mouse Deer was supposed to be smart!

NARRATOR 1: *(to other NARRATORS and audience)* But Mouse Deer didn't put in his leg. Instead, he picked up a stick with his mouth and put in one end.

CROCODILE: *Chomp!*

NARRATOR 4: Crocodile grabbed the stick and pulled it underwater.

NARRATOR 2: Mouse Deer laughed.

MOUSE DEER: *(laughs)* Stupid Crocodile! Don't you know a stick from a leg?

NARRATOR 3: And he ran off to drink somewhere else!

* * *

NARRATOR 1: Another day, Mouse Deer went back to the river.

NARRATOR 4: All he saw there was a floating log.

NARRATOR 2: But he knew Crocodile looked like a log when he floated.

NARRATOR 3: Mouse Deer had an idea. He said out loud,

MOUSE DEER: *(to himself, but loud and clear)* If that log is really Crocodile, it won't talk. But if it's really just a log, it will tell me. *(freezes till NARRATOR 1 speaks again)*

NARRATOR 3: *(to NARRATOR 1 and others)* Hold everything! Mouse Deer said Crocodile would be quiet but a log would *say* something?

NARRATOR 2: Now, that's really dumb!

NARRATOR 4: It sure is!

NARRATOR 1: *(to other NARRATORS and audience)* But then Mouse Deer *listened.*

NARRATOR 4: A rough voice said,

CROCODILE: *(low and growly)* I'm really just a log.

NARRATOR 2: Mouse Deer laughed.

MOUSE DEER: *(laughs)* Stupid Crocodile! Do you think a log can talk?

NARRATOR 3: And off he ran again!

* * *

NARRATOR 1: Another day, Mouse Deer wanted to *cross* the river.

NARRATOR 4: He wanted to eat tasty fruits and roots and shoots on the other *side.*

NARRATOR 2: But he didn't want Crocodile to eat him first!

NARRATOR 3: Mouse Deer had an idea. He called out,

MOUSE DEER: *(brightly)* Crocodile! *(freezes till NARRATOR 1 speaks again)*

NARRATOR 2: *(to NARRATOR 1 and others)* I don't believe this!

NARRATOR 4: Mouse Deer *called* for Crocodile?

NARRATOR 3: How dumb can he get!

NARRATOR 1: *(to other NARRATORS and audience)* But then Crocodile rose from the water.

CROCODILE: *(low and growly)* Hello, Mouse Deer. Have you come to be my breakfast?

MOUSE DEER: Not today, Crocodile. I have orders from the King. He wants me to count all the crocodiles.

CROCODILE: *(very impressed)* The King! Tell us what to do.

MOUSE DEER: You must line up from *this* side of the river to the *other* side.

NARRATOR 4: Crocodile got all his friends and family. They lined up across the river.

NARRATOR 2: Mouse Deer jumped onto Crocodile's back.

MOUSE DEER: One.

NARRATOR 3: He jumped onto the next crocodile.

MOUSE DEER: Two.

NARRATOR 1: And the next.

MOUSE DEER: Three.

NARRATOR 4: Mouse Deer kept jumping till he jumped off . . .

NARRATOR 2: on the other side of the river.

CROCODILE: *(calling across the river)* How many are there?

MOUSE DEER: *(calling back)* Just enough! And all stupid!

NARRATOR 3: Then he went off singing his song.

MOUSE DEER: *(to audience)*

    I'm quick and smart as I can be.
    Try and try, but you can't catch me!

NARRATOR 1: In our last story, Mouse Deer meets his most dangerous enemy of all. *(to other NARRATORS)* Can you guess who it is?

NARRATOR 3: Cobra!

NARRATOR 1: No.

NARRATOR 2: Lion!

NARRATOR 1: No.

NARRATOR 4: Tyrannosaur!

NARRATOR 1: No! This one is called,

MOUSE DEER: *(brightly, to audience)* Mouse Deer . . .

NARRATOR 1: and

FARMER: *(pleasantly, to audience)* . . . Farmer.

NARRATORS 2, 3, & 4: *(confused, to audience)* Huh?

NARRATOR 1: Mouse Deer loved to eat the fruits and roots and shoots of the forest. But he loved something else even more.

NARRATOR 4: He loved the vegetables in Farmer's garden.

NARRATOR 2: One day, Mouse Deer went to the edge of the forest.

NARRATOR 3: He looked out at row after row of vegetables.

MOUSE DEER: *(to himself)* Mmmm. Juicy cucumbers! Yummy yams!

NARRATOR 1: He started into the garden.

NARRATOR 4: *Snap!*

MOUSE DEER: *(in pain and shock, looking at his leg)* Oh!

NARRATOR 4: His leg was caught in a snare!

NARRATOR 2: Mouse Deer pulled and pulled.

NARRATOR 3: But he could not get away.

MOUSE DEER: Oh, no! Farmer will have me for dinner!

NARRATOR 1: Then he saw Farmer coming. Mouse Deer thought fast.

MOUSE DEER: *(makes a face like he's thinking hard, then brightens)*

NARRATOR 4: He lay on the ground and made his body stiff.

FARMER: *(pleasantly, to himself)* Well, well. Look what I caught. A mouse deer! *(looks closer)* But he looks dead.

NARRATOR 2: Farmer pushed him with his foot.

NARRATOR 3: Mouse Deer didn't move.

FARMER: Maybe he's been dead a long time. Too bad! I guess we can't eat him.

NARRATOR 1: He pulled Mouse Deer's leg out of the snare. Then he tossed Mouse Deer back into the forest.

NARRATOR 4: Mouse Deer landed with a soft *plop*. Then he jumped up and ran.

FARMER: *(calling after him angrily)* Hey! You tricked me!

NARRATOR 2: Mouse Deer laughed.

MOUSE DEER: *(laughs, then to audience)* Farmer is smart. But Mouse Deer is smarter!

* * *

NARRATOR 1: A few days passed. Mouse Deer kept thinking about all those vegetables.

NARRATOR 4: One day, he went back to the edge of the forest.

MOUSE DEER: *(to himself)* Mmmm. Tasty gourds! Scrumptious sweet potatoes!

NARRATOR 2: Then he saw something new.

NARRATOR 3: It looked like a man. But its head was a coconut, and its body was rubber.

MOUSE DEER: A scarecrow! That silly Farmer. Does he think he can scare me with that? I'll show him how scared I am!

NARRATOR 1: Mouse Deer marched up to the scarecrow. He gave it a big kick.

MOUSE DEER: Take *this*! *("kicks" it with one hand, as a hoof)*

NARRATOR 4: But his leg stuck to the scarecrow. The scarecrow was covered with sticky sap from a rubber tree!

MOUSE DEER: Let me go! *(grunts as he struggles)*

NARRATOR 2: He pulled and he pulled. Then he pushed with his other front leg.

MOUSE DEER: *(grunts as he pushes forward with other hand/hoof)*

NARRATOR 3: That leg stuck too.

MOUSE DEER: *Turn me loose! (grunts as he struggles)*

NARRATOR 1: He pulled and he pulled. Then he pushed with his two back legs.

MOUSE DEER: *(grunts as he hops forward on both feet/hooves)*

NARRATOR 4: They stuck too.

MOUSE DEER: PUT ME DOWN! *(grunts as he struggles)*

NARRATOR 2: He pulled and he pushed and he pulled and he pushed.

NARRATOR 3: But Mouse Deer was trapped.

MOUSE DEER: *(stops and pants)*

NARRATOR 1: Then he saw Farmer.

MOUSE DEER: *(gasps)*

NARRATOR 1: Mouse Deer thought fast.

MOUSE DEER: *(thinks hard, then looks shocked and scared)*

NARRATOR 4: But he didn't have any ideas!

FARMER: *(pleasantly)* Well, well. How nice of you to come back.

NARRATOR 2: He pulled Mouse Deer off the scarecrow and carried him to the house.

NARRATOR 3: He put him outside in an empty chicken coop.

FARMER: *(still pleasantly)* I'll keep you here tonight. And tomorrow you'll be our dinner. *(leaves)*

NARRATOR 1: All that night, Mouse Deer couldn't sleep. He didn't want to be dinner!

NARRATOR 4: When the sun rose, Mouse Deer just lay there sadly. Then he heard something.

DOG: *(in a barking voice)* Why, it's Mouse Deer!

MOUSE DEER: *(perks up and looks)*

DOG: So Farmer caught you at last. It serves you right!

NARRATOR 2: It was Farmer's dog.

NARRATOR 3: Mouse Deer thought fast.

MOUSE DEER: *(thinks hard, then brightens)* What do you mean, Dog? Farmer didn't catch me.

DOG: *(suspiciously)* Then why are you in the coop?

MOUSE DEER: Because there aren't enough beds in the house. You see, Farmer is holding a feast tomorrow. And I'm the guest of honor.

DOG: Guest of honor? That's not fair! *I've* been his loyal friend for years, and *you're* just a *thief.* The guest of honor should be *me!*

MOUSE DEER: *(thoughtfully)* You know, Dog, you're right. Why don't you take my place? When Farmer sees you in here, he'll make *you* the guest of honor instead.

DOG: *(surprised)* Really? You don't mind?

MOUSE DEER: Not at all. You deserve it.

DOG: Mouse Deer, you're not so bad after all. Thank you!

NARRATOR 1: Dog lifted the latch and opened the door.

MOUSE DEER: You're welcome, Dog. Enjoy the feast.

NARRATOR 4: Mouse Deer ran for the forest. Then he watched from the forest edge.

NARRATOR 2: He saw Farmer come out and stare at Dog.

NARRATOR 3: Then he heard Farmer yell.

FARMER: You stupid dog! You let the mouse deer get away!

NARRATOR 1: Mouse Deer laughed.

MOUSE DEER: *(laughs, then to audience)* Farmer will have to find a *different* dinner now!

NARRATOR 4: Then he went off singing his song.

MOUSE DEER: *(to audience)*

    I'm quick and smart as I can be.
    Try and try, but you can't catch me!

NARRATOR 1: And there they are—three stories about Mouse Deer. *(to other NARRATORS) Now* do you believe in him?

NARRATORS 2, 3, & 4: *(look at each other)*

NARRATOR 3: Well . . . .

NARRATOR 2: Uh . . . .

NARRATOR 4: We guess so, but . . . .

MOUSE DEER: *(to all NARRATORS)* Hey! Who are *you*?

NARRATOR 1: Hi, Mouse Deer. We're the narrators. We help tell the stories.

NARRATOR 3: That's right!

MOUSE DEER: Help tell . . . ?! Hey, are you trying to trick me?

NARRATOR 4: No!

NARRATOR 2: No!

MOUSE DEER: Well, that's good, and you know why? *(to audience)*
  I'm quick and smart as I can be.
  Try and try, but you can't catch me!

  (waves to audience) Bye, now!

ALL NARRATORS: *(confused, to audience)* Huh?

The Calabash Kids
A Tale of Tanzania

Told by Aaron Shepard

Adapted for reader's theater by the author, from his story appearing in Australia's *School Magazine,* June 1996

> For more reader's theater, visit Aaron Shepard's RT Page at
> **www.aaronshep.com/rt**

PREVIEW: The prayers of a lonely woman are answered when her gourds change into children.

GENRE: Folktales   READERS: 16 or more
CULTURE: African, Tanzanian   READER AGES: 7–11
THEME: Name-calling   LENGTH: 8 minutes

ROLES: Narrators 1–4, Shindo, Chieftain, Children 1–7, (Kitete), Women 1–3

NOTES: This tale comes from the Chagga people, found on the slopes of Mount Kilimanjaro. For best effect, place NARRATORS 1 and 2 at far left, and 3 and 4 at far right, as seen from the audience. The number of roles can be increased by assigning each of the CHILD roles to two or more readers speaking in unison. *Shindo* is pronounced "SHEEN-do" or "SHEE-'n-do," sounding like "she in doe." *Kitete* is pronounced "Kee-TAY-tay," rhyming with "key day day." To hear the names, and for other special features, visit www.aaronshep.com/extras.

NARRATOR 1: Once there was a woman named Shindo, who lived in a village at the foot of a snow-capped mountain.

NARRATOR 4: Her husband had died, and she had no children, so she was very lonely.

NARRATOR 2: And she was always tired too, for she had no one to help with the chores.

NARRATOR 3: All on her own, she

NARRATOR 1: cleaned the hut,

NARRATOR 4: cleaned the yard,

NARRATOR 2: tended the chickens,

NARRATOR 3: washed her clothes in the river,

NARRATOR 1: carried water,

NARRATOR 4: cut firewood,

NARRATOR 2: and cooked her solitary meals.

NARRATOR 3: At the end of each day, Shindo gazed up at the snowy peak and prayed.

SHINDO: Great Mountain Spirit! My work is too hard. Send me help!

NARRATOR 1: One day, Shindo was weeding her small field by the river, where she grew vegetables and bananas and gourds. Suddenly, a noble chieftain appeared beside her.

CHIEFTAIN: I am a messenger from the Great Mountain Spirit.

NARRATOR 4: He handed the astonished woman some gourd seeds.

CHIEFTAIN: Plant these carefully. They are the answer to your prayers.

NARRATOR 2: Then the chieftain vanished.

SHINDO: *(skeptically, looking at the seeds in her hand)* What help could I get from a handful of seeds?

NARRATOR 3: Still, she planted and tended them as carefully as she could.

NARRATOR 1: Shindo was amazed at how quickly the seeds grew. In just a week, long vines trailed over the ground, and ripe gourds hung from them.

NARRATOR 4: Shindo brought the gourds home, sliced off the tops, and scooped out the pulp. Then she laid the gourds on the rafters of her hut to dry.

NARRATOR 2: When they hardened, she could sell them at the market as calabashes, to be made into bowls and jugs.

NARRATOR 3: One fine gourd Shindo set by the cook fire. This one she wanted to use herself, and she hoped it would dry faster.

NARRATOR 1: The next morning, Shindo went off again to tend her field.

NARRATOR 4: But meanwhile, back in the hut,

NARRATOR 2: the gourds began to change.

NARRATOR 3: They sprouted heads,

NARRATOR 1: then arms,

NARRATOR 4: then legs.

NARRATOR 2: Soon they were not gourds at all.

NARRATOR 3: They were—

ALL NARRATORS: children!

NARRATOR 1: One boy lay by the fire, where Shindo had put the fine gourd.

NARRATOR 4: The other children called to him from the rafters.

CHILDREN:

> Ki-te-te, come help us!
> We'll work for our mother.
> Come help us, Ki-te-te,
> Our favorite brother!

NARRATOR 2: Kitete helped his brothers and sisters down from the rafters.

NARRATOR 3: Then the children started quickly on the chores.

CHILD 1: Clean the hut!

CHILD 2: Clean the yard!

CHILD 3: Feed the chickens!

CHILD 4: Wash the clothes!

CHILD 5: Carry water!

CHILD 6: Cut the wood!

CHILD 7: Cook the meal!

NARRATOR 1: All joined in but Kitete.

NARRATOR 4: Drying by the fire had made the boy slow-witted. So he just sat there, smiling widely.

NARRATOR 2: When the work was done, Kitete helped the others climb back on the rafters.

NARRATOR 3: Then they all turned again into gourds.

NARRATOR 1: That afternoon, as Shindo returned home, the other women of the village called to her.

WOMAN 1: Who were those children in your yard today?

WOMAN 2: Where did they come from?

WOMAN 3: Why were they doing your chores?

SHINDO: *(angrily)* What children? Are you all making fun of me?

NARRATOR 4: But when she reached her hut, she was astounded.

NARRATOR 2: The work was done, and even her meal was ready!

NARRATOR 3: She could not imagine who had helped her.

NARRATOR 1: The same thing happened the next day. As soon as Shindo had gone off, the gourds turned into children,

NARRATOR 4: with heads

NARRATOR 2: and arms

NARRATOR 3: and legs.

NARRATOR 1: The ones on the rafters called out,

CHILDREN:

> Ki-te-te, come help us!
> We'll work for our mother.
> Come help us, Ki-te-te,
> Our favorite brother!

NARRATOR 4: Kitete helped them down, and they did all the chores.

CHILD 1: Clean the hut!

CHILD 2: Clean the yard!

CHILD 3: Feed the chickens!

CHILD 4: Wash the clothes!

CHILD 5: Carry water!

CHILD 6: Cut the wood!

CHILD 7: Cook the meal!

NARRATOR 2: Then they climbed back to the rafters, and turned again into gourds.

NARRATOR 3: Once more, Shindo came home and was amazed to see the work all done. But this time, she decided to find out who were her helpers.

NARRATOR 1: The next morning, Shindo pretended to leave, but she hid beside the door of the hut and peeked in. And so she saw the gourds turn into children,

NARRATOR 4: with heads

NARRATOR 2: and arms

NARRATOR 3: and legs.

NARRATOR 1: And she heard the ones on the rafters call out,

CHILDREN:

> Ki-te-te, come help us!
> We'll work for our mother.
> Come help us, Ki-te-te,
> Our favorite brother!

NARRATOR 4: Kitete helped them down. As the children rushed out the door, they nearly ran into Shindo.

NARRATOR 2: She was too astonished to speak, and so were the children. But after a moment, they went on with their chores.

CHILD 1: Clean the hut!

CHILD 2: Clean the yard!

CHILD 3: Feed the chickens!

CHILD 4: Wash the clothes!

CHILD 5: Carry water!

CHILD 6: Cut the wood!

CHILD 7: Cook the meal!

NARRATOR 3: When they were done, they started to climb back to the rafters.

SHINDO: *(urgently)* No, no! You must not change back into gourds! You will be the children I never had, and I will love you and care for you!

* * *

NARRATOR 1: So Shindo kept the children as her own.

NARRATOR 4: She was no longer lonely.

NARRATOR 2: And the children were so helpful, she soon became rich, with many fields of vegetables and bananas, and flocks of sheep and goats.

NARRATOR 3: That is, all were helpful but Kitete, who stayed by the fire with his simple-minded smile.

NARRATOR 1: Most of the time, Shindo didn't mind.

NARRATOR 4: In fact, Kitete was really her favorite, because he was like a sweet baby.

NARRATOR 2: But sometimes, when she was tired or unhappy about something else, she would get annoyed and yell at him.

SHINDO: You useless child! Why can't you be smart like your brothers and sisters, and work as hard as they do?

NARRATOR 3: Kitete would only grin back at her.

NARRATOR 1: One day, Shindo was out in the yard, cutting vegetables for a stew. As she carried the pot from the bright sunlight into the hut, she tripped over Kitete.

NARRATOR 4: She fell, and the clay pot shattered. Vegetables and water streamed everywhere.

SHINDO: *(getting up, screaming at him)* Stupid boy! Haven't I told you to stay out of my way? *(derisively)* But what can I expect? You're not a real child at all. You're nothing but a calabash!

NARRATOR 2: The very next moment, Kitete was no longer there.

NARRATOR 3: In his place was a gourd.

SHINDO: *(shrieking)* What have I done? I didn't mean what I said! You're not a calabash, you're my own darling son!

NARRATOR 1: The other children came crowding into the hut.

SHINDO: Oh, children, please do something!

NARRATOR 4: They looked at each other a moment.

NARRATOR 2: Then over each other they climbed, scampering up to the rafters.

NARRATOR 3: When the last child had been helped up by Shindo, they called out one last time,

CHILDREN:

> Ki-te-te, come help us!
> We'll work for our mother.
> Come help us, Ki-te-te,
> OUR FAVORITE BROTHER!

NARRATOR 1: For a long moment, nothing happened.

NARRATOR 4: Then slowly,

NARRATOR 2: the gourd began to change.

NARRATOR 3: It sprouted a head,

NARRATOR 1: then arms,

NARRATOR 4: then legs.

NARRATOR 2: At last, it was not a gourd at all.

NARRATOR 3: It was—

SHINDO & CHILDREN: *(shouting happily, as SHINDO hugs him)*
Kitete!

* * *

NARRATOR 1: Shindo learned her lesson.

NARRATOR 4: Ever after, she was very careful what she called
her children.

NARRATOR 2: And so they gave her comfort and happiness,

NARRATOR 3: all the rest of her days.

The Hidden One
A Native American Legend

Told by Aaron Shepard

Adapted for reader's theater by the author, from his story appearing in *Cricket,*
Oct. 1998

PREVIEW: The invisible hunter at the end of the village is sought as husband by every village maiden—but will Little Scarface even dare to try?

GENRE: Folktales, Cinderella tales
CULTURE: Native American, Canadian
THEME: Self-esteem, heroines

READERS: 13
READER AGES: 7 and up
LENGTH: 8 minutes

ROLES: Narrators 1–4, Little Scarface, Sister, Father, Patient One, Hidden One, Boy, Young Man, Old Woman, Young Woman

NOTES: This tale comes from the Mi'kmaq (or Micmac) tribe of Nova Scotia, New Brunswick, and Prince Edward Island, Canada. Two picture books of other versions are *Sootface: An Ojibwa Cinderella Story,* retold by Robert D. San Souci, illustrated by Daniel San Souci, Delacorte, New York, 1994; and *The Rough-Face Girl,* retold by Rafe Martin, illustrated by David Shannon, Putnam, New York, 1992. For best effect, place NARRATORS 1 and 2 at far left, and 3 and 4 at far right, as seen from the audience. For special features, visit www.aaronshep.com/extras.

NARRATOR 1: A long time ago, in a village by a lake, there lived a great hunter who was invisible. He was called the Hidden One. It was known that any young woman who could see him would become his bride.

NARRATOR 4: Many were the hopeful young women who visited his wigwam at the far end of the village. Each was tested by the hunter's sister, who was called the Patient One. But years passed, and none succeeded.

NARRATOR 2: In the same village lived two sisters who had lost their mother. The younger sister had a good heart, but the older one was jealous and cruel.

NARRATOR 3: While their father was out hunting, the older sister would torment the younger one, holding her down and burning her arms and face with sticks from the fire. Then she would tell her,

SISTER: Don't you dare tell our father, or next time will be worse!

NARRATOR 1: When the father came home, he would ask in dismay,

FATHER: Why is she burnt again?

NARRATOR 4: The older sister would answer,

SISTER: The stupid, clumsy thing! She was playing with the fire, just like you told her not to!

NARRATOR 2: The father would turn to the younger.

FATHER: *(incredulously)* Is this true?

NARRATOR 3: But she only bit her lip and said nothing.

NARRATOR 1: After a while she had so many scars, she was called Little Scarface. She lost her long braids too, when her sister singed them off.

NARRATOR 4: And she had to go barefoot and wear rags, for her sister would not allow her any animal skins to make moccasins or new clothes.

NARRATOR 2: Of course, the sister made up all different reasons to tell their father.

NARRATOR 3: And he would shake his head in sorrow and disappointment.

NARRATOR 1: One day, the older sister put on her finest clothes and many shiny strings of shell beads. She asked Little Scarface,

SISTER: *(snootily)* Do you know what *I'm* doing? *I'm* going to marry the *Hidden* One. Of course, that's something *you* could never *dream* of.

NARRATOR 4: Little Scarface bowed her head.

NARRATOR 2: When the older sister reached the wigwam at the edge of the village, she was greeted by the sister of the hunter. The Patient One told her,

PATIENT ONE: You are welcome. My brother will return soon from the hunt. Come help me prepare the evening meal.

NARRATOR 3: The two of them worked awhile, till the sun was nearly down. Then the Patient One led the young woman to the lake.

NARRATOR 1: She pointed along the shore.

PATIENT ONE: *(pointing past the sister)* My brother comes. Do you see him?

NARRATOR 4: The young woman saw no one, but she had decided to pretend.

SISTER: Of course. *(pointing)* There he is now!

NARRATOR 2: The eyes of the Patient One narrowed.

PATIENT ONE: *(suspiciously)* And what is his shoulder strap?

SISTER: A strip of rawhide.

NARRATOR 3: . . . said the young woman, thinking it a safe guess.

NARRATOR 1: The Patient One frowned.

PATIENT ONE: Let us return to the wigwam.

NARRATOR 4: They had just finished making the meal when a deep voice said,

HIDDEN ONE: Greetings, my sister.

NARRATOR 2: The young woman jumped in surprise.

NARRATOR 3: She stared at the entrance but saw no one.

PATIENT ONE: Greetings, my brother.

NARRATOR 1: As the young woman watched with wide eyes, a moccasin appeared in mid-air and dropped to the floor, followed by another.

NARRATOR 4: A moment later, bits of food were rising from a birch-bark tray near the fire and vanishing into an invisible mouth.

NARRATOR 2: The young woman turned to the Patient One.

SISTER: *(cheerily)* When will our wedding take place?

PATIENT ONE: *(turning on her angrily)* What wedding? Do you think my brother would marry a liar and a fool?

NARRATOR 3: The young woman ran crying from the wigwam.

NARRATOR 1: All the next morning she stayed in bed, weeping and sobbing.

NARRATOR 4: Then Little Scarface came to her.

LITTLE SCARFACE: *(softly)* Sister, let me have skins to make moccasins and new clothes. It is my turn to visit the Hidden One.

SISTER: *(screaming)* How dare you!

NARRATOR 2: The sister jumped up and slapped Little Scarface, knocking her to the floor.

SISTER: Are you so *stupid* to think you can do what I *couldn't?* Even if you *saw* him, do you think he'd marry a pathetic thing like *you?*

NARRATOR 3: She sank back to the bed in tears.

NARRATOR 1: Little Scarface sat huddled for a long time, listening to her sister howl and sob. Then she rose and said again,

LITTLE SCARFACE: *(still softly)* It is my turn to visit the Hidden One.

NARRATOR 4: Her sister stopped crying and stared in amazement.

NARRATOR 2: Little Scarface went to her father's chest and took out an old pair of moccasins. She put them on her own small feet.

NARRATOR 3: Then she went out into the woods. She chose a birch tree and carefully stripped off the bark in a single sheet. From this she made a suit of clothes, which she put on in place of her rags. Then she started back through the village.

BOY: *(pointing)* Look at Little Scarface!

NARRATOR 1: . . . yelled a boy.

BOY: She's dressed like a tree!

YOUNG MAN: Hey, Little Scarface!

NARRATOR 4: . . . a young man called.

YOUNG MAN: Are those moccasins big enough for you?

OLD WOMAN: I don't believe it!

NARRATOR 2: . . . an old woman said.

OLD WOMAN: She's on her way to the Hidden One!

YOUNG WOMAN: Oh, Little Scarface,

NARRATOR 3: . . . called a young woman,

YOUNG WOMAN: did you burn yourself and cut off your hair to look pretty for him?

NARRATOR 1: Ignoring their taunts and laughter, Little Scarface walked on till she reached the wigwam at the village edge.

NARRATOR 4: The Patient One regarded the young woman with surprise but told her,

PATIENT ONE: You are welcome.

NARRATOR 2: Little Scarface helped prepare the evening meal. When the sun was nearly down, the Patient One led her to the lake. She told her,

PATIENT ONE: *(pointing)* My brother comes. Do you see him?

NARRATOR 3: Little Scarface gazed along the shore.

LITTLE SCARFACE: *(looking hard)* I'm not sure. . . .

NARRATOR 1: Then her eyes lit in wonder.

LITTLE SCARFACE: Yes, I see him! But how can there *be* such a one?

NARRATOR 4: The Patient One looked at her curiously.

PATIENT ONE: What is his shoulder strap?

LITTLE SCARFACE: His shoulder strap is . . . is the Rainbow!

NARRATOR 2: The Patient One's eyes grew wide.

PATIENT ONE: And his bowstring?

LITTLE SCARFACE: His bowstring is . . . the Milky Way!

NARRATOR 3: The Patient One smiled.

PATIENT ONE: Let us return.

NARRATOR 1: When they reached the wigwam, the Patient One took the strange clothes off Little Scarface and washed her with water from a special jar.

NARRATOR 4: The young woman's scars disappeared, leaving her skin shining and smooth.

NARRATOR 2: A magic comb made the young woman's hair grow quickly to her waist, ready for braiding.

NARRATOR 3: Then the Patient One opened a chest and took out a beautiful wedding outfit. Little Scarface had just put it on when a deep voice said,

HIDDEN ONE: Greetings, my sister.

NARRATOR 1: Little Scarface turned to the entrance and stared at the magnificent young hunter.

NARRATOR 4: As their eyes met, she saw the surprise in his.

PATIENT ONE: *(smiling)* Greetings, my brother. You are discovered!

NARRATOR 2: The Hidden One walked over to Little Scarface and took her hands in his.

HIDDEN ONE: *(with deep feeling)* For years I have waited to find a woman of pure heart and brave spirit. Only such a one could see me. And now you shall be my bride.

NARRATOR 3: So they were married.

NARRATOR 1: And from then on, Little Scarface had a *new* name—

NARRATOR 4: the Lovely One.

NARRATOR 2: For she too had been hidden,

NARRATOR 3: and now was hidden no more.

The Boy Who Wanted the Willies

Told by Aaron Shepard

Adapted for reader's theater by the author

For more reader's theater, visit Aaron Shepard's RT Page at
www.aaronshep.com/rt

PREVIEW: Hans has never in his life been frightened—but a night in a haunted castle should finally give him his chance.

GENRE: Folktales, tall tales, ghost stories
CULTURE: German, European
THEME: Fearlessness
READERS: 19 or more
READER AGES: 8–12
LENGTH: 10 minutes

ROLES: Narrators 1–4, Hans, Sister, Father, Mother, Strangers 1 & 2, King, Vampire, Werewolf, Skeletons 1–4, Giant, Princess, (Other Family), (Other Strangers), (Other Skeletons), (3 Sons)

NOTES: The story of the fearless lad in the haunted castle is well known throughout Europe, and is found in North America as well. This retelling is based on the version from the Brothers Grimm—but with a lot of liberties taken. For best effect, place NARRATORS 1 and 2 at far left, and 3 and 4 at far right, as seen from the audience. For special features, visit www.aaronshep.com/extras.

NARRATOR 1: There was once a boy who was never frightened—for he had not enough sense to be scared.

HANS: *(cheerfully, to audience)* That's me!

NARRATOR 4: One day, Hans and his big sister were walking home after dark.

NARRATOR 2: The wind howled, and the trees creaked and groaned. The road led past a graveyard, where the moon lit up rows of tombstones.

NARRATOR 3: Hans's sister began to quiver and quake.

SISTER: Ooh! This place gives me the willies!

HANS: The willies? What are the willies?

SISTER: *(scornfully)* Do I have to tell you everything? The willies are when you get so scared, you shiver and shake.

HANS: Well! I never had anything like that! I wish *I* would get the willies, so I'd know what they're like.

SISTER: *(to audience, shakes her head in disgust)*

NARRATOR 1: The more Hans thought it over, the more he wondered about the willies, and the more he wished he could have them. One day he told himself,

HANS: *(to audience)* If I want the willies, I'd better go look for them.

NARRATOR 4: So he said good-bye to his family—

HANS: *(waves and smiles)*

SISTER: What a fool!

FATHER: I can't believe he's my son!

MOTHER: Or mine!

NARRATOR 4: —and he started down the road.

NARRATOR 2: Hans walked for many days. Everyone he met, he asked,

HANS: *(to all STRANGERS)* Can you give me the willies?

NARRATOR 3: Many tried—

ALL STRANGERS: *(try to scare HANS with scary faces and spooky sounds)*

HANS: *(looks bored and sighs)*

NARRATOR 3: —but none could.

ALL STRANGERS: *(shrug to audience)*

NARRATOR 1: At last he came to the King's castle and stood before the King.

HANS: Your Majesty, can *you* give me the willies?

KING: Of course I can. I'm the King!

NARRATOR 4: The King waved his royal scepter.

KING: *(waving his scepter, then pointing it at HANS)* I command you to have . . . the willies!

NARRATOR 2: Hans waited,

NARRATOR 3: but nothing happened.

HANS: I'm sorry, Your Majesty, I still don't have them.

KING: Oh well, at least I know where you can get them. On the other side of my kingdom is a haunted castle. If you spend the night there, you are sure to get the willies.

HANS: Thank you, Your Majesty!

KING: There's just one problem. No one who goes there ever lives through the night. *(cheerfully)* But, if you stay alive and break the spell, you'll find the castle treasure!

HANS: That's fine with me, as long as I get the willies!

KING: *(to audience, gives a look of disbelief)*

NARRATOR 1: It was midnight when Hans reached the castle. The towers cast eerie shadows under the full moon.

NARRATOR 4: The drawbridge lowered itself at Hans's feet. *Creeeeeeeeeeeek. Booooom.*

HANS: *(happily, to audience)* Seems like a friendly place!

NARRATOR 2: As Hans entered the great hall, a fire sprang to life in the huge fireplace. *Voooooom!*

NARRATOR 3: Hans pulled up a chair and settled himself to wait.

HANS: *(cheerfully, to audience)* Now I'm *sure* to get the willies.

NARRATOR 1: The clock in the great hall struck one. *Bonnngggggg.*

NARRATOR 4: A voice boomed out behind him.

VAMPIRE: Velcome!

NARRATOR 2: Hans looked around and saw two men playing cards. One had a long, black cloak, and the other had a furry face.

WEREWOLF: *(growls at HANS and bares his teeth)*

VAMPIRE: *(to HANS)* Vould you care to join our game? It's been so long since ve had anyvun to . . . play vith.

NARRATOR 3: Hans took a seat.

HANS: Certainly! It will pass the time, while I'm waiting for the willies!

VAMPIRE: I vill explain the rules. If my furry friend vins . . . he vill rip you to shreds.

WEREWOLF: *(snarls at HANS)*

VAMPIRE: If I vin . . . I vill drink your blood. If you vin . . . ve vill let you live.

HANS: Sounds fair to me!

WEREWOLF: *(growls)*

NARRATOR 1: The furry man dealt the cards.

NARRATOR 4: They played for almost an hour.

NARRATOR 2: In the end, the cloaked man won.

VAMPIRE: *(laughs ominously)* I vant to drink your blood!

NARRATOR 3: He moved closer to Hans, showing two long, pointy teeth.

HANS: I think you cheated.

NARRATOR 1: Hans reached for the pointy teeth and broke them off— *Snap!*

VAMPIRE: YEEE-OWWWWWWWW!

NARRATOR 4: And out of the hall ran the man.

WEREWOLF: *(roars)*

NARRATOR 2: The furry man leaped at Hans, but Hans sprang away and the man flew past—right out an open window.

WEREWOLF: *(screams)*

NARRATOR 3: Hans heard a dull *thud.* Then he went and settled himself again before the fire.

HANS: *(to audience)* I enjoyed the game, but when do I get the willies?

NARRATOR 1: The clock struck two. *Bonnngggggg. Bonnngggggg.*

NARRATOR 4: Hans heard a rattling, and into the hall marched a long line of skeletons.

NARRATOR 2: The first skeleton snapped its fingers. *Click. Click.*

SKELETON 1: *(with NARRATOR, starts snapping fingers)*

NARRATOR 3: The second skeleton knocked its knees. *Clack. Clack.*

SKELETON 2: *(with NARRATOR, starts knocking knees together)*

NARRATOR 1: The third skeleton drummed its skull. *Clock. Clock.*

SKELETON 3: *(with NARRATOR, starts pretending to knock on head)*

NARRATOR 4: The fourth skeleton tapped along its ribs in a little tune. *Clackety, click clock. Clackety, click clock.*

SKELETON 4: *(with NARRATOR, starts tapping ribs)*

HANS: Nice beat!

SKELETONS 1–4: *(keep "playing")*

NARRATOR 2: The other skeletons formed a circle and started to dance. One skeleton stretched a hand toward Hans.

HANS: Don't mind if I do!

NARRATOR 3: Hans took hold of two bony hands and danced in the circle around the hall.

HANS: *(dances in place, with arms outstretched)* Hey, this is fun!

SKELETONS 1–4: *(play faster)*

NARRATOR 1: The music got faster. *Clackety, clackety, click clock clackety. Clackety, clackety, click clock clackety.*

HANS: *(dancing faster)* Hold it, I can't dance that fast!

SKELETONS 1–4: *(play even faster)*

NARRATOR 4: But the skeletons gripped his hands harder and danced even faster. *Clackety clickety, clackety clockety. Clackety clickety, clackety clockety.*

HANS: *(dancing even faster)* I said HOLD IT! *(stops, digs in)*

NARRATOR 2: Hans gave a yank and—*Pop!*—the two skeletons' arms came right off.

SKELETONS 1–4: *(freeze)*

NARRATOR 3: The music and the dancing stopped.

HANS: *(sheepishly, holding up the arms)* I think you lost something.

NARRATOR 1: The skeletons rushed at Hans and started jumping on him. Hans grabbed a chair and swung it, this way and that. *Crash! Bash!*

NARRATOR 4: Bones flew here, there, and everywhere, till the skeletons lay all in pieces on the floor.

NARRATOR 2: Hans gathered them up and tossed them out the window.

NARRATOR 3: Then he settled himself once again before the fire.

HANS: *(to audience)* I like a little dancing, but I wonder when I'm going to get those willies!

NARRATOR 1: The clock struck three. *Bonnngggggg. Bonnngggggg. Bonnngggggg.*

NARRATOR 4: From up the chimney came a deep voice.

GIANT: LOOK OUT BELOOOOOOOWWW!

NARRATOR 2: Something huge came falling down, swerved to miss the fire, and—*thump*—landed before the fireplace.

NARRATOR 3: It was a giant body, with no arms or legs or head.

GIANT: *(still from up the chimney)* LOOK OUT BELOOOOOOOWWW!

NARRATOR 1: *Thump thump thump thump.*

NARRATOR 4: Two giant legs and two giant arms landed next to it.

GIANT: LOOK OUT BELOOOOOOOWWW!

NARRATOR 2: *Thump.*

NARRATOR 3: A giant head landed by the rest.

HANS: *(to the audience)* I get it! It's a puzzle, and I have to put it together!

NARRATOR 1: Hans heaved the two giant legs and stuck them onto the body. *Snap. Snap.*

GIANT: *(angrily)* Hey!

NARRATOR 4: It was the giant head talking.

GIANT: You got the shoes pointing out!

HANS: Oh, sorry.

NARRATOR 2: He switched the legs. *Snap. Snap. Snap. Snap.*

NARRATOR 3: Then he stuck on the arms and the head. *Snap. Snap. Snap.*

NARRATOR 1: The giant jumped up.

GIANT: The spell is broken! You're the only one ever to get me together. The others all died of fright long before this! Now follow me to the castle treasure.

NARRATOR 4: Hans followed him to the doorway.

GIANT: *(brusquely, gesturing out)* You first.

HANS: *(graciously, also gesturing out)* After *you*.

NARRATOR 2: The giant led him to the courtyard and pointed to a shovel under a tree.

GIANT: *(pointing)* Dig there!

HANS: *(irritated, also pointing) You* dig there!

NARRATOR 3: The giant dug till he uncovered three pots of gold.

GIANT: *(pointing his thumb back)* Take them inside!

HANS: *(really annoyed, also pointing his thumb back) You* take them inside!

NARRATOR 1: The giant took the pots of gold and set them down in the great hall.

GIANT: *(pointing to one pot, then another, then at HANS)* One is for the king, one is for the poor, and one is for you.

NARRATOR 4: Then he fell into pieces again and flew up the chimney—

NARRATOR 2: first the head, then the arms and legs, then the giant body.

HANS: *(to audience)* Some folks just can't keep things together.

NARRATOR 3: Hans went back to his chair before the fire, curled up in it, and sighed.

HANS: *(to audience)* It's nice to be rich, but when will I *ever* get the willies?

* * *

NARRATOR 1: And that is how Hans stayed alive, broke the spell, and found the treasure.

NARRATOR 4: When the King heard the tale, he let Hans live in the castle, and when Hans grew up, he married the King's daughter.

NARRATOR 2: Within a year they had triplets—

NARRATOR 3: three fine sons.

PRINCESS: Dearest, would you like to name them?

HANS: Certainly! Their names are Willy . . . Willy . . . and Willy!

PRINCESS: *(confused)* But why all the same?

HANS: *(triumphantly, to audience)* Because now I'll have the Willies!

ALL (except Hans): *(to audience, give a look of disbelief and dismay)*

The Princess Mouse
A Tale of Finland

Told by Aaron Shepard

Adapted for reader's theater by the author, from his picture book published by Atheneum, New York, 2003

PREVIEW: When a young man seeks a wife by way of family tradition, he finds himself engaged to a mouse.

GENRE: Folktales   READERS: 8 or more
CULTURE: Finnish   READER AGES: 8–12
THEME: Kindness, humility, integrity   LENGTH: 12 minutes

ROLES: Narrators 1–4, Mikko, Princess Mouse, Farmer, Brother, (Other Mice/Wedding Guests/Servants), (Rats/Horses), (Coachman), (Footman), (Brother's Sweetheart)

NOTES: For best effect, place NARRATORS 1 and 2 at far left, and 3 and 4 at far right, as seen from the audience. In scenes between MIKKO and PRINCESS MOUSE, they can suggest their size difference if she looks up and he looks down as they face diagonally or toward the audience. Below is the tune for "The Song of the Princess Mouse," an original composition. To hear the music, and for other special features, visit www.aaronshep.com/extras.

NARRATOR 1: Once there was a farmer with two sons. One morning he said to them,

FARMER: Boys, you're old enough now to marry. But in our family, we have our own way to choose a bride.

NARRATOR 4: The younger son nodded and listened respectfully, but the older one said,

BROTHER: *(rudely)* You've told us, Father. We must each cut down a tree and see where it points.

FARMER: That's right. Then walk that way till you find a sweetheart. That's how we've done it, and that's how we always will.

NARRATOR 2: Now, the older son already knew who he wanted to marry. He also knew how to cut a tree so it fell how he wanted. So, his tree fell and pointed to the farm where his sweetheart lived.

NARRATOR 3: The younger son, whose name was Mikko, didn't have a sweetheart, but he thought he'd try his luck in the town. Well, maybe he cut the tree wrong, or maybe it had thoughts of its own, but it fell pointing to the forest.

BROTHER: *(mockingly)* Good job, Mikko! What sweetheart will you find there? A wolf or a fox?

MIKKO: *(bristling)* Never mind. I'll find who I find.

NARRATOR 1: The two young men went their ways. Mikko walked through the forest for hours without seeing a soul. But at last he came to a cottage deep in the woods.

MIKKO: I knew I'd find a sweetheart!

NARRATOR 4: But when he went inside, he saw no one.

MIKKO: *(sadly)* All this way for nothing.

PRINCESS MOUSE: Maybe not!

NARRATOR 2: Mikko looked around, but the only living thing in sight was a little mouse on a table. Standing on its hind legs, it gazed at him with large, bright eyes.

MIKKO: Did you say something?

PRINCESS MOUSE: Of course I did! Now, why don't you tell me your name and what you came for?

NARRATOR 3: Mikko had never talked with a mouse, but he felt it only polite to reply.

MIKKO: My name is Mikko, and I've come looking for a sweetheart.

PRINCESS MOUSE: *(squeals in delight)* Why, Mikko, I'll gladly be your sweetheart!

MIKKO: *(confused)* But you're only a mouse.

PRINCESS MOUSE: That may be true, but I can still love you faithfully. Besides, even a mouse can be special! Come feel my fur.

NARRATOR 1: With one finger, Mikko stroked the mouse's back.

MIKKO: *(in surprise)* Why, it feels like velvet! Just like the gown of a princess!

PRINCESS MOUSE: That's right, Mikko.

NARRATOR 4: And as he petted her, she sang to him prettily.

PRINCESS MOUSE:

> Mikko's sweetheart will I be.
> What a fine young man is he!
> Gown of velvet I do wear,
> Like a princess fine and rare.

NARRATOR 2: Mikko looked into those large, bright eyes and thought she really was quite nice, for a mouse. And since he'd found no one else anyway, he said,

MIKKO: *(kindly)* All right, little mouse, you can be my sweetheart.

PRINCESS MOUSE: *(happily)* Oh, Mikko! I promise you won't be sorry.

NARRATOR 3: Mikko wasn't so sure, but he just stroked her fur and smiled.

NARRATOR 1: When Mikko got home, his brother was already there boasting to their father.

BROTHER: My sweetheart has rosy red cheeks and long golden hair.

FARMER: Sounds very nice. And what about yours, Mikko?

BROTHER: *(laughing meanly)* Yes, Mikko. Did you find a sweetheart with a nice fur coat? *(keeps chuckling)*

NARRATOR 4: Now, Mikko didn't want to admit his sweetheart was a mouse. So he said,

MIKKO: Mine wears a velvet gown, like a princess!

BROTHER: *(gasps)*

NARRATOR 2: His brother stopped laughing.

NARRATOR 3: The farmer said,

FARMER: Well! It sounds like Mikko's tree pointed a good way too! But now I must test both your sweethearts. Tomorrow you'll ask them to weave you some cloth, then you'll bring it home to me. That's how we've done it, and that's how we always will.

NARRATOR 1: They started out early next morning. When Mikko reached the cottage in the woods, there was the little mouse on the table, jumping up and down in happiness.

PRINCESS MOUSE: Oh, Mikko, I'm so glad you're here! Is this the day of our wedding?

NARRATOR 4: Mikko sighed and gently stroked her fur.

MIKKO: *(glumly)* Not yet, little mouse.

PRINCESS MOUSE: Why, Mikko, you look so sad! What's wrong?

MIKKO: My father wants you to weave some cloth. But how can you do that? You're only a mouse!

PRINCESS MOUSE: That may be true, but I'm also your sweetheart, and surely Mikko's sweetheart can weave! But you must be tired from your walk. Why don't you rest while I work?

MIKKO: *(yawning)* All right.

NARRATOR 2: Mikko lay down on a bed in the corner, and the little mouse sang him a pretty lullaby.

PRINCESS MOUSE:

> Mikko's sweetheart will I be.
> What a fine young man is he!
> Cloth of linen I will weave.
> I'll be done when he must leave.

NARRATOR 3: When the little mouse was sure that Mikko was asleep, she picked up a sleigh bell on a cord and rang it.

NARRATOR 1: Out of mouseholes all around the room poured hundreds of mice.

NARRATOR 4: They all stood before the table, gazing up at her.

PRINCESS MOUSE: Hurry! Each of you, fetch a strand of the finest flax.

NARRATOR 2: The mice rushed from the cottage.

NARRATOR 3: Then one, two, three, and back they were, each with a strand of flax.

NARRATOR 1: First they spun it into yarn on the spinning wheel.

NARRATORS 2–4 (or OTHER MICE): *Whirr. Whirr. Whirr.*

NARRATOR 4: Some worked the pedal,

NARRATOR 2: some fed the flax,

NARRATOR 3: some rode around with the wheel.

NARRATOR 1: Then they strung the yarn on the loom and wove it into cloth.

NARRATORS 2–4 (or OTHER MICE): *Swish. Thunk. Swish. Thunk. Swish. Thunk.*

NARRATOR 4: Some worked the pedals,

NARRATOR 2: some rocked the beater,

NARRATOR 3: some sailed the shuttle back and forth.

NARRATOR 1: At last they cut the cloth from the loom and tucked it in a nutshell.

PRINCESS: Now, off with you!

NARRATOR 4: And they all scampered back to their mouseholes.

PRINCESS MOUSE: *(calling)* Mikko, wake up! It's time to go home! And here is something for your father.

NARRATOR 2: Mikko sleepily took the nutshell.

NARRATOR 3: He didn't know why his father should want such a thing, but he said,

MIKKO: Thank you, little mouse.

NARRATOR 1: When he got home, his brother was proudly presenting the cloth from his sweetheart. The farmer looked it over.

FARMER: Strong and fairly even. Good enough for simple folks like us. And where is yours, Mikko?

NARRATOR 4: Mikko blushed and handed him the nutshell.

BROTHER: *(scornfully)* Look at that! Mikko asked for cloth, and his sweetheart gave him a nut!

NARRATOR 2: But the farmer opened the nutshell and peered inside. Then he pinched at something and started to pull. Out came linen, fine beyond belief. It *kept* coming too, yard after yard after yard.

NARRATOR 3: Mikko's brother gaped with open mouth, and Mikko did too!

FARMER: There can be no better weaver than Mikko's sweetheart! But both your sweethearts will do just fine. Tomorrow you'll bring them home for the wedding. That's how we've done it, and that's how we always will.

NARRATOR 1: When Mikko arrived at the cottage next morning, the little mouse again jumped up and down.

PRINCESS MOUSE: Oh, Mikko, is this the day of our wedding?

MIKKO: *(glumly)* It is, little mouse.

NARRATOR 4: But he sounded more glum than ever.

PRINCESS MOUSE: Why, Mikko, what's wrong?

MIKKO: *(blurting out in distress)* How can I bring home a mouse to marry? My brother and father and all our friends and neighbors will laugh and think I'm a fool!

PRINCESS MOUSE: *(softly) They* might think so, indeed. But, Mikko, what do *you* think?

NARRATOR 2: Mikko looked at the little mouse, gazing at him so seriously with her large, bright eyes.

NARRATOR 3: He thought about how she loved him and cared for him.

MIKKO: *(decisively)* I think you're as sweet as any sweetheart could be. So let them laugh and think what they like. Today you'll be my bride.

PRINCESS MOUSE: Oh, Mikko, you've made me the happiest mouse in the world!

NARRATOR 1: She rang her sleigh bell, and to Mikko's astonishment, a little carriage raced into the room.

NARRATOR 4: It was made from a nutshell and pulled by four black rats. A mouse coachman sat in front, and a mouse footman behind.

PRINCESS MOUSE: Mikko, aren't you going to help me down?

NARRATOR 2: Mikko lifted her from the table and set her in the carriage. The rats took off and the carriage sped from the cottage, so that Mikko had to rush to catch up.

NARRATOR 3: While he hurried along behind her, the little mouse sang a pretty song.

PRINCESS MOUSE:

> Mikko's sweetheart will I be.
> What a fine young man is he!
> In a carriage I will ride
> When I go to be his bride.

NARRATOR 1: At last they reached the farm and then the spot for the wedding, on the bank of a lovely, swift-flowing stream.

NARRATOR 4: The guests were already there enjoying themselves. But as Mikko came up, they all grew silent and stared at the little carriage.

NARRATOR 2: Mikko's brother stood with his bride, gaping in disbelief. Mikko and the little mouse went up to him.

BROTHER: *(loudly)* That's the stupidest thing I ever saw.

NARRATOR 3: And with one quick kick, he sent the carriage, the rats, and the mice, all into the stream. Before Mikko could do a thing, the current bore them away.

MIKKO: *(beside himself)* What have you done! You've killed my sweetheart!

BROTHER: Are you crazy? That was only a mouse!

MIKKO: *(defiantly but near tears)* She may have been a mouse, but she was also my sweetheart, and I really did love her!

NARRATOR 1: He was about to swing at his brother, when his father called out.

FARMER: Mikko, look!

NARRATOR 4: All the guests were staring downstream and pointing and crying out in wonder.

NARRATOR 2: Mikko turned and to his amazement saw four black horses pulling a carriage out of the stream.

NARRATOR 3: A coachman sat in front and a footman behind, and inside was a soaked but lovely princess in a gown of pearly velvet.

NARRATOR 1: The carriage rode up along the bank and stopped right before him.

PRINCESS MOUSE: Mikko, aren't you going to help me down?

NARRATOR 4: Mikko stared blankly a moment, and then his eyes flew wide.

MIKKO: Are you the little mouse?

PRINCESS MOUSE: *(laughing)* I surely was, but no longer. A witch enchanted me, and the spell could be broken only by one brother who wanted to marry me and another who wanted to kill me. But, sweetheart, I need a change of clothes. I can't be wet at our wedding!

NARRATOR 2: And a grand wedding it was, with Mikko's bride the wonder of all. The farmer could hardly stop looking at her.

NARRATOR 3: Of course, Mikko's brother was a bit jealous, but his own bride was really quite nice, so he couldn't feel too bad.

NARRATOR 1: The next day, the princess brought Mikko back to her cottage—

NARRATOR 4: but it was a cottage no longer!

NARRATOR 2: It was a castle with hundreds of servants,

NARRATOR 3: and there they made their home happily.

NARRATOR 1: And if Mikko and the princess had any sons,

ALL: you know just how they chose their brides.

The Legend of Slappy Hooper
An American Tall Tale

Told by Aaron Shepard

Adapted for reader's theater by the author, from his picture book published by Scribners, New York, 1993

> For more reader's theater, visit Aaron Shepard's RT Page at
> **www.aaronshep.com/rt**

PREVIEW: Slappy is the world's biggest, fastest, bestest sign painter, but he's *too good*—his pictures keep coming to life.

GENRE: Tall tales, folktales
CULTURE: American
THEME: Pursuit of excellence

READERS: 8 or more
READER AGES: 8–13
LENGTH: 10 minutes

ROLES: Narrators 1–3, Slappy, Rose Red, Baldwin Eagle, Ray Sunshine, Michael, (Vacationers), (Firefighters)

NOTES: The legend of "Slappy Hooper, World's Biggest, Fastest, and Bestest Sign Painter" was collected in Chicago in 1938 by Jack Conroy for the Federal Writers' Project of the Works Progress Administration. It was first published in B. A. Botkin's *A Treasury of American Folklore,* Crown, New York, 1944. This is a free retelling. For special features, visit www.aaronshep.com/extras.

NARRATOR 1: You've heard about Paul Bunyan, the greatest lumberjack of all time.

NARRATOR 3: And you've heard about Pecos Bill, the greatest cowboy.

NARRATOR 2: Now let us tell you about the world's

NARRATOR 1: biggest,

NARRATOR 2: fastest,

NARRATOR 3: bestest

NARRATOR 2: sign painter.

SLAPPY: *(proudly, to audience, in booming voice)* That's me!
Slappy Hooper!

NARRATOR 1: You'd better believe Slappy was biggest! Why, he was
seven feet tall with shoulders to match, and he weighed three hundred
pounds, even without his cap and coverall and brush and bucket.

NARRATOR 2: And fastest?

SLAPPY: Just give me an eight-inch brush! *(slaps paint on a wall)*

NARRATOR 1: *Slip!*

NARRATOR 2: *Slop!*

NARRATOR 3: *Slap!*

NARRATOR 2: The job was done.

SLAPPY: And so smooth, you'd never see a brush stroke.

NARRATOR 3: And you bet Slappy was bestest! That was on account
of his pictures.

SLAPPY: No one else ever made them so true to life!

NARRATOR 3: In fact, some folks said they were *too* true to life.

NARRATOR 1: Slappy's trouble started with the huge red rose he
painted on the sign for Rose's Florist Shop.

ROSE RED: Slappy, it's so real!

NARRATOR 1: . . . said Miss Rose Red, the owner.

ROSE RED: Why, I can just about smell the fragrance!

NARRATOR 2: But a week later, Rose Red fluttered into Slappy's sign shop.

ROSE RED: Slappy, that sign of yours was *too good.*

SLAPPY: *(puzzled) Too* good?

ROSE RED: That's right! The bees got wind of it and swarmed all over that rose, trying to get in. They scared away all my customers! That was bad enough, but wait till you see what's happened now!

NARRATOR 3: When they reached the florist shop, Slappy saw that the bees were gone. But the rose had withered and died!

ROSE RED: No one buys from a florist with a withered flower on her sign. That's the last thing you'll paint for *me,* Slappy Hooper!

NARRATOR 1: The story got around, but most folks just laughed, and they still wanted Slappy to do their signs.

NARRATOR 2: His next job was to paint a billboard for the Eagle Messenger Service. Slappy painted an eagle three times larger than life.

BALDWIN EAGLE: Amazing!

NARRATOR 2: . . . said Mr. Baldwin Eagle.

BALDWIN EAGLE: It's so real, I could swear I saw it blink! Wait a minute. I *did* see it blink!

NARRATOR 3: Then the bird flapped its wings and flew right off the billboard!

BALDWIN EAGLE: That sign was *too good.* That's the last time you'll work for *me,* Slappy Hooper!

NARRATOR 1: Folks were getting scared to hire Slappy. But at last he got a job from the Sunshine Travel Agency.

NARRATOR 2: The billboard was to show a man and woman on a beach, toasting under a hot sun. Slappy painted it the day after a big snowstorm.

RAY SUNSHINE: Wonderful!

NARRATOR 3: . . . said Mr. Ray Sunshine.

RAY SUNSHINE: Why, that sun makes me feel hot! And look! The snow on the sidewalk is melting!

NARRATOR 3: But a couple of days later, Slappy got a call.

RAY SUNSHINE: Slappy, your sign is *too good.* Get down here right away!

NARRATOR 1: When Slappy arrived, he saw that the sidewalk and street in front of the billboard were covered with beach chairs. People sat around in swimsuits and sunglasses, sipping lemonade and splashing suntan lotion.

RAY SUNSHINE: They're blocking traffic, and the mayor blames me! Besides, they won't need my travel agency if they take their vacations here! You've got to *do* something, Slappy.

NARRATOR 2: So Slappy set up his gear and got to work. He painted the sun on the billboard much hotter. Before long, the crowd was sweating buckets and complaining of sunburn. Then everyone packed up and left.

RAY SUNSHINE: Good work, Slappy! *(gasps and points)* Look at that!

NARRATOR 2: The man and woman on the *billboard* were walking off, too!

NARRATOR 3: Just then, a lick of flame shot up the wall of the building across the street. Slappy's sign had set it on fire! In a few minutes, fire trucks clanged up and firefighters turned hoses on the flames.

RAY SUNSHINE: Slappy! Try something else!

NARRATOR 1: Slappy got back to work. He painted a storm cloud across that sun. But he had to jump clear when the cloud shot bolts of lightning!

NARRATOR 2: Then the storm broke.

NARRATOR 3: Slappy's cloud rained so hard, the billboard overflowed and flooded all of Main Street!

RAY SUNSHINE: *Never again,* Slappy Hooper!

NARRATOR 1: After that, no one *on earth* would hire Slappy. It looked as if his sign-painting days were done.

NARRATOR 2: Slappy felt so low, he made up his mind to throw his paint kit in the river. He dragged it onto the tallest bridge in town and was just about to chuck it, when a voice thundered out beside him.

MICHAEL: Don't dump that gear, Slappy. You're going to need it!

NARRATOR 3: Right next to Slappy stood a man almost as big as Slappy himself. He wore a paint-splotched white coverall and a cap with two little angel wings sticking out. He carried an eight-inch brush.

SLAPPY: Who are *you*?

MICHAEL: I'm Michael, from the Heavenly Sign Company. The Boss has had an eye on you for some time, Slappy, and He likes your work. He's got a job for you—if you don't mind working in the rain.

SLAPPY: Tell me about it.

MICHAEL: We need someone to paint a rainbow this Wednesday. Most of the time, we handle all the rainbows ourselves. But it's going to rain in a bunch of places Wednesday, and we could sure use some help.

SLAPPY: I'm your man.

NARRATOR 3: . . . said Slappy.

NARRATOR 1: That Wednesday morning, Slappy rented a cannon, and set it in a big cow pasture. He tied two ropes to his scaffold, then ran the other ends through a couple of skyhooks. Then he loaded the skyhooks in the cannon and shot them straight up.

SLAPPY: *BOOM! (looks up)*

NARRATOR 1: Sure enough, the skyhooks caught on the sky.

NARRATOR 2: Slappy felt the first raindrops. He piled all his paints and brushes onto his scaffold, climbed on, and hoisted himself up, up, and up! He kept going till he was just under the clouds. Then he tied his ropes and started to paint.

NARRATOR 1: *Slip!*

NARRATOR 2: *Slop!*

NARRATOR 3: *Slap!*

NARRATOR 2: He had only just finished, when the sun popped through the clouds and lit up what he'd done.

NARRATOR 3: There never was a finer rainbow! It had every color you could imagine, each one blending perfectly with the next.

SLAPPY: *(proudly, looking over his work)* And not a brush stroke in sight!

NARRATOR 1: Just then, Slappy felt a big jolt. He looked up to see what had caused it.

SLAPPY: Oh, no!

NARRATOR 1: The sun had run smack into his skyhooks!

NARRATOR 2: Slappy shut his eyes and waited for the long drop to the ground. But it never came. When Slappy looked again, he saw why.

SLAPPY: *(amazed)* For heaven's sake!

NARRATOR 2: Slappy's hooks had caught on the sun itself! And the sun was pulling his rig across the sky!

NARRATOR 3: Now, another sign painter might have been frightened. But not Slappy Hooper! He was enjoying the ride!

NARRATOR 1: He'd covered a good distance when Michael appeared on the scaffold beside him.

MICHAEL: *(thundering)* The Boss liked your rainbow, Slappy.

SLAPPY: You mean, it wasn't *too good*?

MICHAEL: If it isn't *too good,* it's not good enough! That's how *we* figure. Anyhow, now that you're here, the Boss has another job for you—if you don't mind working odd hours.

SLAPPY: Tell me about it.

MICHAEL: It's the sunrise and sunset. I guess you know, the Boss Himself has been painting them since time began. But He's done it so long, He'd like to give someone else a chance.

SLAPPY: I'm your man.

NARRATOR 3: . . . said Slappy Hooper.

NARRATOR 1: Slappy's been up there ever since.

NARRATOR 2: Of course, you can't see him, with the sun so bright— but he's there all the same.

NARRATOR 3: Night and day, the sun pulls Slappy and his rig around the world. And every time Slappy comes to a horizon, he reaches up with his eight-inch brush.

NARRATOR 1: *Slip!*

NARRATOR 2: *Slop!*

NARRATOR 3: *Slap!*

NARRATOR 2: The job is done.

SLAPPY: *(to audience)* And never a brush stroke in sight!

The Gifts of Wali Dad
A Tale of India and Pakistan

Told by Aaron Shepard

Adapted for reader's theater by the author, from his picture book published by Atheneum, New York, 1995

For more reader's theater, visit Aaron Shepard's RT Page at
www.aaronshep.com/rt

PREVIEW: Wali Dad, a humble grass-cutter, never asked for wealth—so why can't he give it away?

GENRE: Folktales
CULTURE: Asian Indian, Pakistani
THEME: Generosity

READERS: 15
READER AGES: 8–13
LENGTH: 10 minutes

ROLES: Narrators 1–4, Wali Dad, Merchant, Queen, King, Ministers 1 & 2, Peris 1 & 2, Servants 1–3

NOTES: For best effect, place NARRATORS 1 and 2 at far left, and 3 and 4 at far right, as seen from the audience. *Wali Dad* rhymes with "Wally Todd." *Paisa,* the smallest Indian coin, is pronounced "PAY-sa," sounding like "pace a." *Khaistan* is pronounced "KI-ston," rhyming with "iced on." *Nekabad* is pronounced "NEK-a-bod." *Peri* sounds like "Perry." Peris are an import into India from Persian mythology. Originally considered evil, their image changed gradually to benevolent beings akin to fairies or angels. It is said they feed only on the odor of perfume. To hear the names, and for other special features, visit www.aaronshep.com/extras.

NARRATOR 1: In a mud hut far from town lived an old grass-cutter named Wali Dad.

NARRATOR 4: Every morning, Wali Dad cut and bundled tall, wild grass. Every afternoon, he sold it as fodder in the marketplace.

NARRATOR 2: Each day, he earned thirty paisa. Ten of the small coins went for food. Ten went for clothes and other needs. And ten he saved in a clay pot under his bed.

NARRATOR 3: In this manner Wali Dad lived happily for many years.

NARRATOR 1: One evening, Wali Dad dragged out the pot to see how much money it held. He was amazed to find that his coins had filled it to the brim.

WALI DAD: *(to himself)* What am I to do with all this money? I need nothing more than I have.

NARRATOR 4: Wali Dad thought and thought. At last he had an idea.

NARRATOR 2: The next day, Wali Dad loaded the money into a sack and carried it to a jeweler in the marketplace. He exchanged all his coins for a lovely gold bracelet.

NARRATOR 3: Then Wali Dad visited the home of a traveling merchant.

WALI DAD: Tell me, in all the world, who is the noblest lady?

MERCHANT: Without doubt, it is the young queen of Khaistan. I often visit her palace, just three days' journey to the east.

WALI DAD: Do me a kindness. The next time you pass that way, give her this little bracelet, with my compliments.

NARRATOR 1: The merchant was astonished, but he agreed to do what the ragged grass-cutter asked.

NARRATOR 4: Soon after, the merchant found himself at the palace of the queen of Khaistan. He presented the bracelet to her as a gift from Wali Dad.

QUEEN: *(admiring the bracelet)* How lovely! Your friend must accept a gift in return. My servants will load a camel with the finest silks.

NARRATOR 2: When the merchant arrived back home, he brought the silks to the hut of Wali Dad.

WALI DAD: Oh, no! This is worse than before! What am I to do with such finery?

MERCHANT: Perhaps you could give it to someone else.

NARRATOR 3: Wali Dad thought for a moment.

WALI DAD: Tell me, in all the world, who is the noblest man?

MERCHANT: That is simple. It is the young king of Nekabad. His palace, too, I often visit, just three days' journey to the west.

WALI DAD: Then do me another kindness. On your next trip there, give him these silks, with my compliments.

NARRATOR 1: The merchant was amused, but he agreed.

NARRATOR 4: On his next journey, he presented the silks to the king of Nekabad.

KING: A splendid gift! In return, your friend must have twelve of my finest horses.

NARRATOR 2: So the merchant brought the king's horses to Wali Dad.

WALI DAD: This grows worse and worse! What could I do with twelve horses? *(thinks for a moment)* I know who should have such a gift. I beg you, keep two horses for yourself, and take the rest to the queen of Khaistan!

NARRATOR 3: The merchant thought this was very funny, but he consented. On his next visit to the queen's palace, he gave her the horses.

NARRATOR 1: Now the queen was perplexed. She whispered to her prime minister,

QUEEN: Why does this Wali Dad persist in sending gifts? I have never even heard of him!

MINISTER 1: Why don't you discourage him? Send him a gift so rich, he can never hope to match it.

NARRATOR 4: So in return for the ten horses from Wali Dad, the queen sent back twenty mules loaded with silver.

NARRATOR 2: When the merchant and mules arrived back at the hut, Wali Dad groaned.

WALI DAD: What have I done to deserve this? Friend, spare an old man! Keep two mules and their silver for yourself, and take the rest to the king of Nekabad!

NARRATOR 3: The merchant was getting uneasy, but he could not refuse such a generous offer. So not long after, he found himself presenting the silver-laden mules to the king of Nekabad.

NARRATOR 1: The king, too, was perplexed and asked his prime minister for advice.

MINISTER 2: Perhaps this Wali Dad seeks to prove himself your better. Why not send him a gift he can never surpass?

NARRATOR 4: So the king sent back

NARRATOR 2: twenty camels with golden anklets,

NARRATOR 3: twenty horses with golden bridles and stirrups,

NARRATOR 1: twenty elephants with golden seats mounted on their backs,

NARRATOR 4: and twenty liveried servants to care for them all.

NARRATOR 2: When the merchant guided the servants and animals to Wali Dad's hut, the grass-cutter was beside himself.

WALI DAD: Will bad fortune never end? Please, do not stop for a minute! Keep for yourself two of each animal, and take the rest to the queen of Khaistan!

MERCHANT: *(distressed)* How can I go to her again?

NARRATOR 3: But Wali Dad pleaded so hard, the merchant consented to go just once more.

NARRATOR 1: This time, the queen was stunned by the magnificence of Wali Dad's gift. She turned again to her prime minister.

MINISTER 1: Clearly, the man wishes to marry you. Since his gifts are so fine, perhaps you should meet him!

NARRATOR 4: So the queen ordered a great caravan made ready, with countless horses, camels, and elephants. With the trembling merchant as guide, she and her court set out to visit the great Wali Dad.

NARRATOR 2: On the third day, the caravan made camp, and the queen sent the merchant ahead to tell Wali Dad of her coming. When Wali Dad heard the merchant's news, his head sank to his hands.

WALI DAD: *(mournfully)* Oh, no! Now I will be paid for all my foolishness. I have brought shame on myself, on you, and on the queen. What are we to do?

MERCHANT: I fear we can do nothing!

NARRATOR 3: And the merchant headed back to the caravan.

* * *

NARRATOR 1: The next morning, Wali Dad rose before dawn.

WALI DAD: *(sadly)* Good-bye, old hut. I will never see you again.

NARRATOR 4: The old grass-cutter started down the road. But he had not gone far when he heard a voice.

PERI 1: *(gently)* Where are you going, Wali Dad?

NARRATOR 2: He turned and saw two radiant ladies.

NARRATOR 3: He knew at once they were peris from Paradise.

WALI DAD: *(kneels)* I am a stupid old man. Let me go my way.
I cannot face my shame!

PERI 2: No shame can come to such as you. Though your clothes are poor, in your heart you are a king.

NARRATOR 1: The peri touched him on the shoulder.

NARRATOR 4: To his amazement, he saw his rags turn to fine clothes. A jeweled turban sat on his head. The rusty sickle at his waist was now a gleaming scimitar.

PERI 1: Return, Wali Dad. All is as it should be.

NARRATOR 2: Wali Dad looked behind him. Where his hut had stood, a splendid palace sparkled in the rising sun.

NARRATOR 3: In shock, he turned to the peris, but they had vanished.

NARRATOR 1: Wali Dad hurried back along the road. As he entered the palace, the guards gave a salute. Servants bowed to him, then rushed here and there, preparing for the visitors.

NARRATOR 4: Wali Dad wandered through countless rooms, gaping at riches beyond his imagining.

NARRATOR 2: Suddenly, three servants ran up.

SERVANT 1: *(announcing)* A caravan from the east!

SERVANT 2: No, a caravan from the west!

SERVANT 3: No, caravans from both east *and* west!

NARRATOR 3: The bewildered Wali Dad rushed outside to see two caravans halt before the palace. Coming from the east was a queen in a jeweled litter. Coming from the west was a king on a fine horse.

NARRATOR 1: Wali Dad hurried to the queen.

QUEEN: My dear Wali Dad, we meet at last. *(looks at KING)* But who is that magnificent king?

WALI DAD: I believe it is the king of Nekabad, Your Majesty. Please excuse me for a moment.

NARRATOR 4: He rushed over to the king.

KING: My dear Wali Dad, I had to meet the giver of such fine gifts. *(looks at QUEEN)* But who is that splendid queen?

WALI DAD: *(smiling)* The queen of Khaistan, Your Majesty. Please come and meet her.

NARRATOR 2: And so the king of Nekabad met the queen of Khaistan, and the two fell instantly in love.

NARRATOR 3: A few days later their marriage took place in the palace of Wali Dad. And the celebration went on for many days.

NARRATOR 1: At last Wali Dad had said good-bye to all his guests. The very next morning, he rose before dawn, crept quietly from the palace, and started down the road.

NARRATOR 4: But he had not gone far when he heard a voice.

PERI 1: Where are you going, Wali Dad?

NARRATOR 2: He turned and again saw the two peris.

WALI DAD: *(kneels)* Did I not tell you I am a stupid old man? I should be glad for what I have received, but—

PERI 2: Say no more. You shall have your heart's desire.

NARRATOR 3: And she touched him again.

* * *

NARRATOR 1: So Wali Dad became once more a grass-cutter,

NARRATOR 4: living happily in his hut for the rest of his days.

NARRATOR 2: And though he often thought warmly of his friends the king and queen,

NARRATOR 3: he was careful never to send them another gift.

The Baker's Dozen
A Saint Nicholas Tale

Told by Aaron Shepard

Adapted for reader's theater by the author, from his picture book published by Atheneum, New York, 1995

> For more reader's theater, visit Aaron Shepard's RT Page at
> **www.aaronshep.com/rt**

PREVIEW: Van Amsterdam, the baker, is as honest as he can be—but he may have something left to learn.

GENRE: Legends, St. Nicholas tales
CULTURE: American (Dutch colonial)
THEME: Generosity

READERS: 6 or more
READER AGES: 8–13
LENGTH: 6 minutes

ROLES: Narrators 1–4, Baker, Woman, (Customers), (Children), (Saint Nicholas)

NOTES: For best effect, place NARRATORS 1 and 2 at far left, and 3 and 4 at far right, as seen from the audience. For special features, visit www.aaronshep.com/extras.

NARRATOR 1: In the Dutch colonial town later known as Albany, New York, there lived a baker, Van Amsterdam, who was as honest as he could be.

NARRATOR 4: Each morning, he checked and balanced his scales, and he took great care to give his customers *exactly* what they paid for— not more, and not less.

NARRATOR 2: Van Amsterdam's shop was always busy, because people trusted him, and because he was a good baker as well. And never was the shop busier than in the days before December 6, when the Dutch celebrate Saint Nicholas Day.

NARRATOR 3: At that time of year, people flocked to the baker's shop to buy his fine Saint Nicholas cookies.

NARRATOR 1: Made of gingerbread, iced in red and white, they looked just like Saint Nicholas as the Dutch know him—

NARRATOR 4: tall and thin, with a high, red bishop's cap, and a long, red bishop's cloak.

NARRATOR 2: One Saint Nicholas Day morning, the baker was just ready for business, when the door of his shop flew open.

NARRATOR 3: In walked an old woman, wrapped in a long black shawl.

WOMAN: I have come for a dozen of your Saint Nicholas cookies.

NARRATOR 1: Taking a tray, Van Amsterdam counted out twelve cookies. He started to wrap them, but the woman reached out and stopped him.

WOMAN: I asked for a dozen. You have given me only twelve.

BAKER: Madam, everyone knows that a dozen *is* twelve.

WOMAN: But *I* say a dozen is *thirteen.* Give me one more.

NARRATOR 4: Van Amsterdam was not a man to bear foolishness.

BAKER: Madam, my customers get *exactly* what they pay for—not more, and not less.

WOMAN: Then you may keep the cookies.

NARRATOR 2: She turned to go, but stopped at the door.

WOMAN: Van Amsterdam! However honest you may be, your heart is small and your fist is tight. *Fall again, mount again, learn how to count again!*

NARRATOR 3: Then she was gone.

NARRATOR 1: From that day, everything went wrong in Van Amsterdam's bakery.

NARRATOR 4: His bread rose too high or not at all.

NARRATOR 2: His pies were sour or too sweet.

NARRATOR 3: His cakes crumbled or were chewy.

NARRATOR 1: His cookies were burnt or doughy.

NARRATOR 4: His customers soon noticed the difference. Before long, most of them were going to other bakers.

BAKER: *(to himself)* That old woman has bewitched me. Is this how my honesty is rewarded?

NARRATOR 2: A year passed.

NARRATOR 3: The baker grew poorer and poorer.

NARRATOR 1: Since he sold little, he baked little, and his shelves were nearly bare. His last few customers slipped away.

NARRATOR 4: Finally, on the day before Saint Nicholas Day, not one customer came to Van Amsterdam's shop.

NARRATOR 2: At day's end, the baker sat alone, staring at his unsold Saint Nicholas cookies.

BAKER: I wish Saint Nicholas could help me now.

NARRATOR 3: Then he closed his shop and went sadly to bed.

NARRATOR 1: That night, the baker had a dream. He was a boy again, one in a crowd of happy children. And there in the midst of them was Saint Nicholas himself.

NARRATOR 4: The bishop's white horse stood beside him, its baskets filled with gifts. Nicholas pulled out one gift after another, and handed them to the children.

NARRATOR 2: But Van Amsterdam noticed something strange. No matter how many presents Nicholas passed out, there were always more to give.

NARRATOR 3: In fact, the more he took from the baskets, the more they seemed to hold.

NARRATOR 1: Then Nicholas handed a gift to Van Amsterdam. It was one of the baker's own Saint Nicholas cookies!

NARRATOR 4: Van Amsterdam looked up to thank him, but it was no longer Saint Nicholas standing there.

NARRATOR 2: Smiling down at him was the old woman with the long black shawl.

NARRATOR 3: Van Amsterdam awoke with a start. Moonlight shone through the half-closed shutters as he lay there, thinking.

BAKER: I always give my customers *exactly* what they pay for—not more, and not less. But why *not* give more?

NARRATOR 1: The next morning, Saint Nicholas Day, the baker rose early.

NARRATOR 4: He mixed his gingerbread dough and rolled it out.

NARRATOR 2: He cut the shapes and baked them.

NARRATOR 3: He iced them in red and white to look just like Saint Nicholas.

NARRATOR 1: And the cookies were as fine as any he had made.

NARRATOR 4: Van Amsterdam had just finished, when the door flew open. In walked the old woman with the long black shawl.

WOMAN: I have come for a dozen of your Saint Nicholas cookies.

NARRATOR 2: In great excitement, Van Amsterdam counted out twelve cookies—

NARRATOR 3: and one more.

BAKER: In this shop, from now on, a dozen is thirteen.

WOMAN: You have learned to count well. You will surely be rewarded.

NARRATOR 1: She paid for the cookies and started out. But as the door swung shut, the baker's eyes seemed to play a trick on him.

NARRATOR 4: He thought he glimpsed the tail end of a long red cloak.

* * *

NARRATOR 2: As the old woman foretold, Van Amsterdam *was* rewarded. When people heard he counted thirteen as a dozen, he had more customers than ever.

NARRATOR 3: In fact, Van Amsterdam grew so wealthy that the other bakers in town began doing the same.

NARRATOR 1: From there, the practice spread to other towns, and at last through all the American colonies.

NARRATOR 4: And this, they say, is how thirteen became the "baker's dozen"—

NARRATOR 2: a custom common for over a century,

NARRATOR 3: and alive in some places to this day.

Master Maid
A Tale of Norway

Told by Aaron Shepard

Adapted for reader's theater by the author, from his picture book published by Dial, New York, 1997

For more reader's theater, visit Aaron Shepard's RT Page at
www.aaronshep.com/rt

PREVIEW: When Leif goes to work for the troll, only the advice of a remarkable young woman can save him from his foolishness—if only he'll listen!

GENRE: Folktales, tall tales
CULTURE: Norwegian
THEME: Stubbornness, heroines
READERS: 9 or more
READER AGES: 8–15
LENGTH: 12 minutes

ROLES: Narrators 1–4, Leif, Troll, Master Maid, Father, Fairy, (Stallion), (Forest Chewer), (Mountain Cruncher), (Water Sucker), (Minister)

NOTES: For best effect, place NARRATORS 1 and 2 at far left, and 3 and 4 at far right, as seen from the audience. *Leif* sounds like "lay" with an added *f. Maid* is short here for *maiden,* and *Master Maid* is a Norwegian way of saying "Supergirl." To hear the names, and for other special features, visit www.aaronshep.com/extras.

NARRATOR 1: Once there was a lad named Leif.

NARRATOR 4: Now, Leif was a likeable fellow, and handsome to boot.

NARRATOR 2: But he never wanted to listen to anyone,

NARRATOR 3: and he always had to do things his own way.

NARRATOR 1: His father told him,

FATHER: My son, it's good to make up your own mind. But it's also good to know when others know more than you.

NARRATOR 4: Now, Leif didn't want to hear that either, so he said,

LEIF: Father, I'm going out into the world, where I can do things just as I like.

NARRATOR 2: His father begged Leif not to go, but the more he pleaded, the more Leif was set on it. Finally his father said,

FATHER: Your stubbornness is bound to land you in trouble. But at least take this piece of advice. Whatever you do, *don't go to work for the troll.*

NARRATOR 3: So where do you think Leif went? Right to the house of the troll!

NARRATOR 1: Leif knocked on the door, and the troll himself answered it.

NARRATOR 4: He was huge, and a good deal uglier than anyone you'd care to meet.

LEIF: Pardon me, sir. I'm looking for work.

TROLL: Are you, now?

NARRATOR 2: . . . said the troll, feeling the boy's arm.

TROLL: I could use a fellow like you.

NARRATOR 3: The troll led him into the stable and said,

TROLL: I'm taking my goats to pasture. Since it's your first day, I won't ask much of you. Just shovel out all this dung.

LEIF: Well, that's kind of you, sir. You're surely easy to please!

TROLL: But just one thing. Don't go looking through the rooms of the house, or you won't live to tell about it. *(leaves)*

NARRATOR 1: When the troll had gone, Leif said to himself,

LEIF: Not look through the house? Why, that's *just* what I want to do!

NARRATOR 4: So Leif went through all the rooms till he came to the kitchen. And there stirring a big iron pot was the loveliest maiden he had ever seen.

MASTER MAID: *(shocked)* Good Lord! What are you doing here?

LEIF: I've just got a job with the troll.

MASTER MAID: Then heaven help you get out of it! Weren't you warned about working here?

LEIF: I was, but I'm glad I came anyway, else I never would have met *you.*

NARRATOR 2: Well, the girl liked *that* answer, so they sat down to chat. They talked and talked and talked some more, and before the day was done, he held her hand in his.

NARRATOR 3: Then the girl asked,

MASTER MAID: What did the troll tell you to do today?

LEIF: Something easy. I've only to clear the dung from the stable.

MASTER MAID: Easy to say! But if you use the pitchfork the ordinary way, ten forkfuls will fly in for every one you throw out! Now, here's what you must do. Turn the pitchfork around and shovel with the handle. Then the dung will fly out by itself.

NARRATOR 1: Leif went out to the stable and took up the pitchfork. But he said to himself,

LEIF: That can't be true, what she told me.

NARRATOR 1: . . . and he shoveled the ordinary way.

NARRATOR 4: Within moments, he was up to his neck in dung.

LEIF: I guess her way wouldn't hurt to try!

NARRATOR 2: So he turned the pitchfork around and shoveled with the handle. In no time at all, the dung was all out, and the stable looked like he had scrubbed it.

NARRATOR 3: As Leif started back to the house, the troll came up with the goats.

TROLL: Is the stable clean?

LEIF: Tight and tidy!

NARRATOR 3: . . . and he showed it to him.

TROLL: You never figured this out for yourself! Have you been talking to my Master Maid?

LEIF: Master Maid? Now, what sort of thing might that be, sir?

TROLL: You'll find out soon enough.

* * *

NARRATOR 1: The next morning, the troll was again to go off with his goats. He told Leif,

TROLL: Today I'll give you another easy job. Just go up the hill to the pasture and fetch my stallion.

LEIF: Thank you, sir. That won't be any trouble.

TROLL: But mind you stay out of the rooms of the house, or I'll make an end of you. *(leaves)*

NARRATOR 4: When the troll had gone off, Leif went right to the kitchen and sat down again with the girl the troll had called Master Maid.

MASTER MAID: Didn't the troll threaten you against coming here?

LEIF: He did, but he'll have to do worse, to keep me away from *you.*

NARRATOR 2: So they talked and talked and talked some more, and before the day was done, he had his arm around her.

NARRATOR 3: Then Master Maid asked,

MASTER MAID: What work did the troll give you today?

LEIF: Nothing hard. I just have to fetch his stallion from the hillside.

MASTER MAID: Yes, but how will you manage? It will charge at you, shooting flame from its mouth and nostrils! But here's how to do it. Take that bridle hanging by the door and hold it before you as you get near. Then the stallion will be tame as a pussycat.

NARRATOR 1: So Leif threw the bridle over his shoulder and went up the hill to the pasture. But he said to himself,

LEIF: That horse looks gentle enough.

NARRATOR 1: . . . and he started right over to it.

NARRATOR 4: As soon as the stallion saw him, it charged at him, shooting flame just as Master Maid had said.

NARRATOR 2: Barely in time, Leif got the bridle off his shoulder and held it before him. The stallion stopped, as tame as you please, and Leif bridled it and rode it back to the stable.

NARRATOR 3: On his way out, he met the troll coming home with the goats.

TROLL: Did you bring home the stallion?

LEIF: Safe and sound!

NARRATOR 3: . . . and he showed him.

TROLL: You never figured this out for yourself! Have you been talking to my Master Maid?

LEIF: Master Maid? Didn't you mention that yesterday? I'd certainly like to know what it is!

TROLL: All in good time.

* * *

NARRATOR 1: The next morning, before the troll left with the goats, he said,

TROLL: I want you to go to the mountain today and collect my tunnel tax from the fairies.

LEIF: All right, sir. I'm sure I can figure it out.

TROLL: But just keep out of the rooms of the house, or you won't make it through another day. *(leaves)*

NARRATOR 4: As soon as the troll had left, off went Leif to the kitchen and once more sat down with Master Maid.

MASTER MAID: Aren't you the least bit afraid of the troll?

LEIF: I am, but not near as much as I'm in love with *you.*

NARRATOR 2: So they talked and talked and talked some more, and before the day was done, she gave him a nice big kiss.

NARRATOR 3: Then Master Maid asked,

MASTER MAID: What are you to do for the troll today?

LEIF: Something simple. I'm to go to the mountain and collect the tunnel tax from the fairies.

MASTER MAID: Simple if you know how! You're lucky I'm here to tell you! Take that club that's leaning against the wall and strike it against the mountain. The rock will open up, and a fairy will ask you how much you want. Be sure to say, "Just as much as I can carry."

NARRATOR 1: So Leif took the club to the mountain and struck it against the side. The rock split wide open, and out came one of the fairies. Through the crack, Leif could see piles and piles of silver, gold, and gems.

LEIF: I've come for the troll's tunnel tax.

FAIRY: How much do you want?

NARRATOR 1: . . . asked the fairy.

NARRATOR 4: Now, Leif figured it wouldn't hurt to ask for extra and then keep some for himself. So he said,

LEIF: As much as you can give me.

NARRATOR 4: As soon as he said it, silver, gold, and gems came streaming out of the mountain and piled up around him. In a few moments he was nearly buried, but the treasure kept coming.

LEIF: I've changed my mind! Just as much as I can carry!

NARRATOR 2: The pile of treasure flew back into the mountain, and the fairy handed him a sack.

NARRATOR 3: As Leif arrived back, he met the troll.

TROLL: Did you collect my tax?

LEIF: Done and delivered!

NARRATOR 3: He opened the sack, and silver, gold, and gems overflowed onto the ground.

TROLL: You never figured this out for yourself! You've been talking with my Master Maid!

LEIF: Master Maid? This is the third time you've spoken of it, sir. I wish I could see it for myself!

TROLL: It won't be long now.

* * *

NARRATOR 1: The next morning, the troll brought Leif to Master Maid.

TROLL: *(to MASTER MAID)* Cut him up and throw him in the stew. And wake me when he's done.

NARRATOR 1: Then he lay down on a bench and started snoring.

NARRATOR 4: Master Maid took a butcher knife down from the wall.

LEIF: You wouldn't!

MASTER MAID: Don't be silly!

NARRATOR 4: She pricked the tip of her little finger and squeezed three drops of blood onto a three-legged stool. Then she put some old rags and shoe soles in the stewpot, along with the kitchen garbage, and a couple of dead rats, and some dung for good measure.

NARRATOR 2: Then she gathered a wooden comb, a lump of salt, and a flask of water.

MASTER MAID: Quick! We must flee while we can!

LEIF: Are you sure we need to rush?

NARRATOR 3: But Master Maid pushed him out the door and over to the stable. They saddled two mares and rode away at full gallop.

NARRATOR 1: Meanwhile, the troll was stirring from his sleep. Without opening his eyes, he called,

TROLL: *(eyes still closed)* Is he ready?

NARRATOR 4: The first drop of blood answered in Master Maid's voice.

MASTER MAID: *(voice only, from offstage)* Tough as leather!

NARRATOR 4: So the troll went back to sleep.

NARRATOR 2: A little later, the troll woke again and called,

TROLL: *(eyes still closed)* Is he cooked?

NARRATOR 3: The second drop of blood said,

MASTER MAID: *(offstage)* Still chewy.

NARRATOR 3: The troll went to sleep again.

NARRATOR 1: At last, the troll woke and called,

TROLL: Isn't he done yet?

NARRATOR 4: The third drop of blood said,

MASTER MAID: *(offstage)* Tender and juicy!

NARRATOR 2: Still half asleep, the troll stumbled over to the pot. He scooped up some stew in a wooden ladle, and took a big mouthful. It was barely in his mouth when he sprayed it across the room.

TROLL: *(spews and sputters)* That little witch!

NARRATOR 2: Then his eyes grew wide.

TROLL: She must have run off with the boy!

NARRATOR 3: The troll raced to the stable and saddled his stallion. Then he rode after them like a whirlwind, with the stallion breathing fire as it went.

NARRATOR 1: In a little while, Leif looked behind and saw the troll chasing them.

LEIF: We're done for!

NARRATOR 4: But Master Maid threw the wooden fork over her shoulder and shouted,

MASTER MAID:

    Fork of wood, bless my soul.
    Turn to trees and stop the troll.

NARRATOR 2: The fork changed to a thick forest that blocked the troll's way. The troll said,

TROLL: I know how to deal with this,

NARRATOR 2: . . . and he called out,

TROLL:

> Forest Chewer, curse her soul.
> Chew the forest, help the troll.

NARRATOR 3: The Forest Chewer appeared out of nowhere and devoured the trees, making a path for the troll's horse.

NARRATOR 1: Leif looked back and again saw the troll.

LEIF: We're lost!

NARRATOR 4: But Master Maid tossed the lump of salt behind her.

MASTER MAID:

> Lump of salt, bless my soul.
> Grow to mountain, stop the troll.

NARRATOR 2: The salt turned to a craggy mountain, and the troll again had to stop.

TROLL: I know how to handle this, too!

> Mountain Cruncher, curse her soul.
> Crunch the mountain, help the troll.

NARRATOR 3: The Mountain Cruncher appeared and bored a tunnel, straight through the mountain.

NARRATOR 1: Meanwhile, Leif and Master Maid came to a sea, where they found a sailboat tied up. They left the horses, boarded the boat, and sailed for the far shore.

NARRATOR 4: They were halfway across when the troll rode up to the water.

TROLL: I can take care of this, as well!

>Water Sucker, curse her soul.
>Suck the water, help the troll.

NARRATOR 2: The Water Sucker appeared and started drinking up the sea.

NARRATOR 3: Soon the boat was scraping bottom.

LEIF: It's the end of us!

NARRATOR 1: But Master Maid took out her flask.

MASTER MAID:

>Drop of water, bless my soul.
>Fill the sea and stop the troll.

NARRATOR 4: She poured overboard a single drop, and the drop of water filled the sea.

TROLL: *(raging at the Water Sucker)* Drink it up! Drink it up!

NARRATOR 2: But not another drop could the Water Sucker drink,

NARRATOR 3: and Leif and Master Maid landed safe on the other shore.

* * *

NARRATOR 1:　It wasn't long then till Leif had Master Maid home, and not long again till they had a wedding.

NARRATOR 4:　But when the minister asked Master Maid if she'd love, honor, and obey, Leif told him,

LEIF:　Never mind that! It's best if *I* obey *her.*

NARRATOR 2:　And he did—

NARRATOR 3:　which is *why* they lived happily ever after.

The Magic Brocade
A Tale of China

Told by Aaron Shepard

Adapted for reader's theater by the author, from his picture book published by Pan Asian/EduStar, Union City, California, 2000

> For more reader's theater, visit Aaron Shepard's RT Page at
> **www.aaronshep.com/rt**

PREVIEW: To save his mother's life, a young man must retrieve her weaving from the fairies of Sun Palace.

GENRE: Folktales   READERS: 9 or more
CULTURE: Chinese   READER AGES: 8–15
THEME: Following dreams; creative process   LENGTH: 12 minutes

ROLES: Narrators 1–4, Widow, Chen (male), Li-en (female), Old Woman, Stall Keeper, (Fairy Ladies)

NOTES: Brocade is woven cloth with raised patterns resembling embroidery. It has been woven in China since at least the third century. There it is used for waistcoats, quilt covers, bedspreads, and other household items. For best effect, place NARRATORS 1 and 2 at far left, and 3 and 4 at far right, as seen from the audience. *Chen* is pronounced "CHEN." *Li-en* is pronounced "lee-EN." To hear the names, and for other special features, visit www.aaronshep.com/extras.

NARRATOR 1: Once in China there lived an old widow and her son, Chen. The widow was known all over for the brocades that she made on her loom.

NARRATOR 4: Weaving threads of silver, gold, and colored silk into her cloth, she made pictures of flowers, birds, and animals—

NARRATOR 2: pictures so real they seemed almost alive.

NARRATOR 3: People said there were no brocades finer than the ones the widow wove.

NARRATOR 1: One day, the widow took a pile of brocades to the marketplace, where she quickly sold them. Then she went about buying her household needs.

NARRATOR 4: All at once she stopped.

WIDOW: Oh, my!

NARRATOR 2: Her eye had been caught by a beautiful painted scroll that hung in one of the stalls.

NARRATOR 3: It showed a marvelous palace, all red and yellow and blue and green, reaching delicately to the sky. All around were fantastic gardens, and walking through them, the loveliest maidens.

NARRATOR 1: The stall keeper asked,

STALL KEEPER: Do you like it? It's a painting of Sun Palace. They say it lies far to the east and is the home of many fairy ladies.

WIDOW: *(sighs)* It's wonderful. It makes me want to be there. *(pays and takes it)*

NARRATOR 4: Though it cost most of her money, the widow could not resist buying the scroll.

NARRATOR 2: When she got back to her cottage, she showed it to her son.

WIDOW: Look, Chen. Have you ever seen anything more beautiful? How I would love to live in that palace, or at least visit it!

NARRATOR 3: Chen looked at her thoughtfully.

CHEN: Mother, why don't you weave the picture as a brocade? That would be almost like being there.

WIDOW: Why, Chen, what a marvelous idea! I'll start at once.

NARRATOR 1: She set up her loom and began to weave.

NARRATOR 4: She worked for hours, then days, then weeks, barely stopping to eat or sleep. Her eyes grew bloodshot, and her fingers raw.

CHEN: *(anxiously)* Mother, shouldn't you get more rest?

WIDOW: Oh, Chen, it's so hard to stop. While I weave, I feel like I'm there at Sun Palace. And I don't want to come away!

NARRATOR 2: Because the widow no longer wove brocades to sell, Chen cut firewood and sold that instead.

NARRATOR 3: Months went by, while inch by inch the pattern appeared on the loom.

NARRATOR 1: One day, Chen came in to find the loom empty and the widow sobbing.

CHEN: *(in alarm)* What's wrong, Mother?

NARRATOR 4: She looked at him tearfully.

WIDOW: *(plaintively)* I finished it.

NARRATOR 2: The brocade was laid out on the floor. And there it all was—the palace reaching to the sky, the beautiful gardens, the lovely fairy ladies.

CHEN: *(in amazement)* It looks so real. I feel like I could step into it!

NARRATOR 3:　Just then, a sudden wind whipped through the cottage. It lifted the brocade, blew it out the window, and carried it through the air.

NARRATOR 1:　The widow and her son rushed outside, only to watch the brocade disappear into the east.

WIDOW:　It's gone!

NARRATOR 4:　And the widow fainted away.

NARRATOR 2:　Chen carried her to her bed and sat beside her for many hours.

NARRATOR 3:　At last her eyes opened.

WIDOW:　*(weakly)* Chen, you must find the brocade and bring it back. I cannot live without it.

CHEN:　Don't worry, Mother. I'll go at once.

NARRATOR 1:　Chen gathered a few things and started to the east.

NARRATOR 4:　He walked for hours, then days, then weeks. But there was no sign of the brocade.

NARRATOR 2:　One day, Chen came upon a lonely hut.

NARRATOR 3:　Sitting by the door was an old, leather-skinned woman smoking a pipe. A horse was grazing nearby.

OLD WOMAN:　Hello, deary. What brings you so far from home?

CHEN:　I'm looking for my mother's brocade. The wind carried it to the east.

OLD WOMAN: Ah, yes. The brocade of Sun Palace! Well, that wind was sent by the fairy ladies of the palace itself. They're using the brocade as a pattern for their weaving.

CHEN: But my mother will die without it!

OLD WOMAN: Well, then, you had best get it back! But you won't get to Sun Palace by foot, so you'd better ride my horse. It will show you the way.

CHEN: Thank you!

OLD WOMAN: Oh, don't thank me yet, deary. Between here and there, you must pass through the flames of Fiery Mountain. If you make a single sound of complaint, you'll be burnt to ashes. After that, you must cross the Icy Sea. The smallest word of discontent, and you'll be frozen solid. *(with a hard look)* Do you still want to go?

CHEN: *(daunted yet determined)* I must get back my mother's brocade.

OLD WOMAN: *(approvingly)* Good boy. Take the horse and go.

NARRATOR 1: Chen climbed on, and the horse broke into a gallop. Before long they came to a mountain all on fire.

NARRATOR 4: Without missing a step, the horse started up the slope, leaping through the flames.

NARRATOR 2: Chen felt the fire singe his skin, but he bit his lip and made not a sound.

NARRATOR 3: At last they came down the other side. When they'd left the flames behind, Chen was surprised to find that his burns were gone.

NARRATOR 1: A little later, they came to a sea filled with great chunks of ice.

NARRATOR 4: Without pausing a moment, the horse began leaping from one ice floe to another.

NARRATOR 2: Waves showered them with icy spray, so that Chen was soaked and shivering. But he held his tongue and said not a word.

NARRATOR 3: Finally they reached the far shore. At once, Chen felt himself dry and warm.

NARRATOR 1: It wasn't long then till they came to Sun Palace. It looked just like his mother's brocade!

NARRATOR 4: He rode to the entrance, sprang from the horse, and hurried into a huge hall.

NARRATOR 2: Sitting there at looms were dozens of fairy ladies, who turned to stare at him, then whispered to each other excitedly. On each loom was a copy of his mother's brocade, and the brocade itself hung in the center of the room.

NARRATOR 3: A lady near the door rose from her loom to meet him.

LI-EN: *(graciously)* My name is Li-en, and I welcome you. You are the first mortal ever to reach our palace. What good fortune brings you here?

NARRATOR 1: The fairy was so beautiful that for a moment Chen could only stare.

NARRATOR 4: Li-en gazed shyly downward.

CHEN: Dear lady, I have come for my mother's brocade.

LI-EN: *(looks up at him in delight)* So you are the widow's son! How we admire that brocade! None of us has been able to match it. We wish to keep it here till we can.

CHEN: But I must bring it home, or my mother will die!

NARRATOR 2: Li-en looked alarmed, and a flurry of whispers arose in the room.

NARRATOR 3: She stepped away to speak softly with several others, then returned to Chen.

LI-EN: We surely must not let that happen to her. Only let us keep the brocade for the rest of the day, so we can try to finish our own. Tomorrow you may take it back with you.

CHEN: *(joyfully)* Thank you, dear lady!

NARRATOR 1: The fairies worked busily to finish their brocades. Chen sat near Li-en at her loom.

NARRATOR 4: As she wove, he told her about his life in the human world, and she told him about hers at Sun Palace. Many smiles and glances passed between them.

NARRATOR 2: When darkness fell, the fairies worked on by the light of a magic pearl.

NARRATOR 3: At last Chen's eyes would stay open no longer, and he drifted to sleep on his chair.

NARRATOR 1: One by one the fairies finished or left off, and went out of the hall.

NARRATOR 4: Li-en was the last one there, and it was almost dawn when she was done. She cut her brocade from the loom and held it beside the widow's.

LI-EN: *(sighs)* Mine is good, but the widow's is still better. If only she could come and teach us herself.

NARRATOR 2: Then Li-en had an idea. With needle and thread, she embroidered a small image onto the widow's brocade—an image of herself on the palace steps.

NARRATOR 3: She softly said a spell. Then she left the hall, with a last long smiling gaze at Chen.

NARRATOR 1: When Chen awoke, the sun was just rising. He looked around the hall for Li-en, but saw no one. Though he longed to find her to say good-bye, he told himself,

CHEN: I must not waste a moment.

NARRATOR 4: He rolled up his mother's brocade, rushed from the hall, and jumped onto the horse.

NARRATOR 2: Back he raced, across the Icy Sea,

NARRATOR 3: and over Fiery Mountain.

NARRATOR 1: When he reached the old woman's hut, she was standing there waiting for him.

OLD WOMAN: Hurry, Chen! Your mother is dying! Put on these shoes, or you'll never get there in time.

NARRATOR 4: Chen put them on.

NARRATOR 2: One step, two, three, then he was racing over the countryside faster than he could believe possible.

NARRATOR 3: In no time, he was home.

NARRATOR 1: He rushed into the cottage and found the widow in bed, pale and quiet.

CHEN: *(in alarm)* Mother!

NARRATOR 4: Her eyes opened slowly.

WIDOW: *(weakly)* Chen?

CHEN: Mother, I brought it.

NARRATOR 2: He unrolled the cloth onto the bed.

WIDOW: My brocade!

NARRATOR 3: The widow raised herself to look. Color came back to her face, and she seemed already stronger.

WIDOW: Chen, I need more light. Let's take it outside.

NARRATOR 1: He helped her out of the cottage and placed the brocade on a rock.

NARRATOR 4: But just then a sudden wind came, and the brocade rose slowly in the air.

NARRATOR 2: It stretched as it rose, growing larger and larger, till it filled their view completely.

NARRATOR 3: The palace was as large as Chen himself had seen it, and standing on the steps was the fairy lady Li-en.

LI-EN: *(beckoning with her hand)* Quickly! While the wind still blows! Step into the brocade!

NARRATOR 1: For a moment, Chen was too astounded to move. Then he took hold of his mother's arm, and together they stepped forward.

NARRATOR 4: There was a shimmering, and there they stood before Sun Palace.

NARRATOR 2: Li-en rushed up to them, and the other fairies gathered around. She said to the widow,

LI-EN: Welcome, honored one. If it pleases you, we wish you to live with us and teach us the secrets of your craft.

WIDOW: *(in amazed delight)* Nothing could please me more! But, Chen, is it all right with you?

NARRATOR 3: Chen looked in Li-en's eyes and smiled.

CHEN: Yes, Mother, it's just fine with me.

NARRATOR 1: So the widow became teacher to the fairies,

NARRATOR 4: and Chen became husband to Li-en.

NARRATOR 2: And people say there are no brocades finer

NARRATOR 3: than the ones they weave at Sun Palace.

Forty Fortunes
A Tale of Iran

Told by Aaron Shepard

Adapted for reader's theater by the author, from his picture book published by Clarion, New York, 1999

For more reader's theater, visit Aaron Shepard's RT Page at
www.aaronshep.com/rt

PREVIEW: When a young man's wife makes him pose as a fortuneteller, his success is unpredictable.

GENRE: Folktales
CULTURE: Iranian (Persian), Middle Eastern
THEME: Pretension

READERS: 11 or more
READER AGES: 8 and up
LENGTH: 10 minutes

ROLES: Narrators 1–4, Ahmed, Jamell, Woman, Minister's Wife, King, Servant, Chief, (Diviners/Thieves/Guards)

NOTES: The story of the would-be fortuneteller is one of the most popular tales of Iran and the rest of the Islamic world. For best effect, place NARRATORS 1 and 2 at far left, and 3 and 4 at far right, as seen from the audience. *Iran* is pronounced "eer-ON," sounding like "ear on." *Isfahan* is pronounced "ISS-fah-hon." *Ahmed* is pronounced "AH-med." *Jamell* is pronounced "ja-MEL." To hear the names, and for other special features, visit www.aaronshep.com/extras.

NARRATOR 1: Once, in the royal city of Isfahan, there lived a young man named Ahmed, who had a wife named Jamell. He knew no special craft or trade, but he had a shovel and a pick—and as he often told his wife,

AHMED: *(cheerfully)* If you can dig a hole, you can always earn enough to stay alive.

NARRATOR 4: That was enough for Ahmed. But it was not enough for Jamell.

NARRATOR 2: One day, as she often did, Jamell went to the public bath to wash herself in the hot pool and chat with the other women. But at the entrance, the woman in charge told her,

WOMAN: You can't come in now. The wife of the King's Royal Diviner is taking the whole place for herself.

JAMELL: *(angrily)* Who does she think she is? Just because her husband tells fortunes!

NARRATOR 3: But all she could do was return home, fuming all the way.

JAMELL: *(furiously)* Ooh!

NARRATOR 1: That evening, when Ahmed handed her his wages for the day, she said,

JAMELL: Look at these few measly coins! I won't put up with this any longer. Tomorrow you'll sit in the marketplace and be a diviner!

AHMED: Jamell, are you insane? What do I know about fortunetelling?

JAMELL: You don't need to know a thing. When anyone brings you a question, you just throw the dice and mumble something that sounds wise. It's either that, or I go home to the house of my father!

NARRATOR 4: So the next day, Ahmed sold his shovel and his pick and bought the dice and the board and the robe of a fortuneteller. Then he sat in the marketplace near the public bath.

NARRATOR 2: Hardly had he gotten settled when there ran up to him the wife of one of the King's ministers.

MINISTER'S WIFE: Diviner, you must help me! I wore my most precious ring to the bath today, and now it's missing. Please, tell me where it is!

NARRATOR 3: Ahmed gulped and cast the dice. As he desperately searched for something wise to say, he happened to glance up at the lady's cloak. There he spied a small hole, and showing through the hole, a bit of her naked arm.

NARRATOR 1: Of course, this was quite improper for a respectable lady, so Ahmed leaned forward and whispered urgently,

AHMED: Madam, I see a hole.

MINISTER'S WIFE: *(leaning closer)* A what?

AHMED: A hole! A hole!

MINISTER'S WIFE: *(perking up)* Of course! A hole!

NARRATOR 4: She rushed back to the bath and found the hole in the wall where she had hidden her ring for safekeeping and forgotten it. Then she came back out to Ahmed.

MINISTER'S WIFE: God be praised! You knew right where it was!

NARRATOR 2: And to Ahmed's amazement, she gave him a gold coin.

AHMED: *(stares at coin in his hand and shakes head in amazement)*

NARRATOR 3: That evening, when Jamell saw the coin and heard the story, she said,

JAMELL: You see? There's nothing to it!

AHMED: God was merciful on this day, but I dare not test Him on another!

JAMELL: Nonsense. If you want to keep your wife, you'll be back in the marketplace tomorrow.

AHMED: *(sighs in resignation)*

NARRATOR 1: Now, it happened that on that very night, at the palace of the King, the royal treasury was robbed.

NARRATOR 4: Forty pairs of hands carried away forty chests of gold and jewels.

NARRATOR 2: The theft was reported next morning to the King. He commanded,

KING: Bring me my Royal Diviner and all his assistants.

NARRATOR 3: But though the fortunetellers cast their dice and mumbled quite wisely, not one could locate the thieves or the treasure.

KING: Frauds! Throw them all in prison!

NARRATOR 1: Now, the King had heard about the fortuneteller who had found the ring of his minister's wife. So he sent two guards to the marketplace to bring Ahmed, who appeared trembling before him.

KING: Diviner, my treasury has been robbed of forty chests. What can you tell me about the thieves?

NARRATOR 4: Ahmed thought quickly about forty chests being carried away.

AHMED: Your Majesty, I can tell you there were . . . forty thieves.

KING: Amazing! None of my own diviners knew as much! But now you must find the thieves and the treasure.

NARRATOR 2: Ahmed felt faint.

AHMED: I'll . . . do my best, Your Majesty, but . . . but it will take some time.

KING: How long?

NARRATOR 3: Ahmed guessed the longest he could get.

AHMED: Uh . . . forty days, Your Majesty. One day for each thief.

KING: A long time indeed! Very well, you shall have it. If you succeed, I'll make you rich. If you don't, you'll rot with the others in prison!

AHMED: *(gasps softly)*

NARRATOR 1: Back home, Ahmed told Jamell,

AHMED: You see the trouble you have caused us? In forty days, the King will lock me away.

JAMELL: Nonsense. Just find the chests like you found the ring.

AHMED: I tell you, Jamell, I found nothing! That was only by the grace of God. But this time there's no hope.

NARRATOR 4: Ahmed took some dried dates, counted out forty, and placed them in a jar.

AHMED: I will eat one of these dates each evening. That will tell me when my forty days are done.

NARRATOR 2: Now, it happened that one of the King's own servants was one of the forty thieves, and he had heard the King speak with Ahmed. That same evening, he hurried to the thieves' meeting place and reported to their chief.

SERVANT: There is a diviner who says he will find the treasure and the thieves in forty days!

CHIEF: He's bluffing. But we can't afford to take chances. Go to his house and find out what you can.

NARRATOR 3: So the servant climbed up to the terrace on the flat roof of Ahmed's house, and he listened down the stairs that led inside.

NARRATOR 1: Just then, Ahmed took the first date from the jar and ate it. He told Jamell,

AHMED: That's one.

SERVANT: *(gasps loudly, nearly falls over)*

NARRATOR 4: The thief was so shocked, he nearly fell down the stairs. He hurried back to the meeting place and told the chief,

SERVANT: This diviner has amazing powers. Without seeing me, he knew I was on the roof! I clearly heard him say, "That's one."

CHIEF: You must have imagined it. Tomorrow night, two of you will go.

NARRATOR 2: So the next night, the servant returned to Ahmed's roof with another of the thieves. As they were listening, Ahmed ate a second date and said,

AHMED: That's two.

NARRATOR 3: The thieves nearly tumbled over each other as they fled the roof and raced back to the chief. The servant told him,

SERVANT: He knew there were two of us! We heard him say, "That's two."

CHIEF: It can't be!

NARRATOR 1: So the night after that, he sent three of the thieves,

NARRATOR 4: and the next night four,

NARRATOR 2: then five,

NARRATOR 3: then six.

NARRATOR 1: And so it went till the fortieth night, when the chief said,

CHIEF: This time, I'll go with you myself.

NARRATOR 4: So all forty thieves climbed up to Ahmed's roof to listen.

NARRATOR 2: Inside, Ahmed gazed at the last date in the jar, then sadly took it out and ate it.

AHMED: That's forty. The number is complete.

NARRATOR 3: Jamell sat beside him.

JAMELL: *(gently)* Ahmed, during these forty days, I've been thinking. I was wrong to make you be a diviner. You are what you are, and I should not have tried to make you something else. Can you forgive me?

AHMED: I forgive you, Jamell, but the fault is mine as well. I should not have done what I knew was not wise. But none of this helps us now.

NARRATOR 1: Just then came a loud banging at the door.

AHMED: *(sighs)* The King's men already!

NARRATOR 4: He went to the door and unbolted it, calling,

AHMED: All right, all right, I know why you're here.

NARRATOR 2: He swung the door open. To his astonishment, he saw forty men kneeling before him and touching their heads to the ground again and again.

CHIEF: Of course you know, O great diviner! Nothing can be hidden from you. But we beg you not to give us away!

NARRATOR 3: Bewildered though he was, Ahmed realized that these must be the thieves. He thought fast and said,

AHMED: Very well, I won't turn you in. But you must replace every bit of the treasure.

CHIEF: At once! At once!

NARRATOR 1: And before the night was through, forty pairs of hands carried forty chests of gold and jewels back into the King's treasury.

NARRATOR 4: Early the next morning, Ahmed appeared before the King.

AHMED: Your Majesty, my magic arts can find either the treasure or the thieves, but not both. Which do you choose?

KING: The treasure, I suppose—though it's a pity not to get the thieves. The boiling oil is all ready for them. Well, never mind. Tell me where the treasure is, and I'll send my men right away.

AHMED: No need, Your Majesty.

NARRATOR 2: Ahmed waved his hand in the air and called,

AHMED: *Pish posh, wish wosh, mish mosh.* By my magic, the chests have returned to their place.

NARRATOR 3: The King himself went with Ahmed to the treasury and found it so.

KING: You are truly the greatest fortuneteller of the age! From this day forth, you shall be my Royal Diviner!

AHMED: *(bowing)* Thank you, Your Majesty, but I'm afraid that's impossible. Finding and restoring your treasure was so difficult, it used up all my powers. I shall never be a diviner again.

KING: What a loss! Then I must doubly reward you. Here, take two of these chests for your own.

NARRATOR 1: So Ahmed returned home to Jamell,

NARRATOR 4: safe,

NARRATOR 2: rich,

NARRATOR 3: and a good deal wiser.

NARRATOR 1: And as any diviner could have foretold,

ALL: they lived happily ever after.

Master Man
A Tall Tale of Nigeria

Told by Aaron Shepard

Adapted for reader's theater by the author, from his picture book published by
HarperCollins, New York, 2001

PREVIEW: Shadusa thinks he's the strongest man in the world—till he meets the *real*
Master Man.

GENRE: Tall tales, folktales
CULTURE: African, Nigerian
THEME: Machismo

READERS: 12 or more
READER AGES: 8 and up
LENGTH: 10 minutes

ROLES: Narrators 1–4, Shadusa, Shettu, Woman, Baby, Master Man, Farmer, Porter, Stranger,
(Other Farmers), (Other Porters)

NOTES: For best effect, place NARRATORS 1 and 2 at far left, and 3 and 4 at far right, as seen
from the audience. BABY's noises can be made partly while others speak. *Shadusa* is pronounced
"sha-DOO-sa," rhyming with "a goose a." *Shettu* is pronounced "SHET-oo," rhyming with "get
two." *Wah* is an African exclamation with no literal meaning. To hear the names, and for other
special features, visit www.aaronshep.com/extras.

NARRATOR 1: Once there was a man who was *strong.*

NARRATOR 4: When he gathered firewood, he hauled twice as much
as anyone else in the village. When he hunted, he carried home two
antelopes at once.

NARRATOR 2: This man's name was Shadusa, and his wife was
named Shettu. One day he said to her,

SHADUSA: *(boastfully, flexing muscles)* Just look at these muscles. I must be the strongest man in the world. From now on, just call me Master Man.

NARRATOR 3: But Shettu said,

SHETTU: *(scolding)* Quit your foolish boasting. No matter how strong you are, there will always be someone stronger. And watch out, or someday you may meet him.

NARRATOR 1: The next day, Shettu paid a visit to a neighboring village. On the walk home she grew thirsty, so she stopped by a well.

NARRATOR 4: She threw in the bucket—

NARRATOR 1: *SPLASH!*

NARRATOR 4: —then she pulled on the rope. But though she tugged and she heaved, she could not lift the bucket.

NARRATOR 2: Just then a woman walked up with a baby strapped to her back.

BABY: *(makes baby noises)*

NARRATOR 3: Balanced on the woman's head was a calabash, a hollow gourd for carrying water. Shettu told her,

SHETTU: *(helpfully)* You'll get no water here today. The bucket won't come up.

NARRATOR 1: The two women pulled together, but still the bucket would not budge.

WOMAN: Wait a moment.

NARRATOR 4: . . . said the woman. She untied her baby and set him on the ground.

WOMAN: *(to BABY)* Pull up the bucket for Mama.

BABY: *(makes baby noises)*

NARRATOR 2: The baby quickly pulled up the bucket and filled his mother's calabash. Then he threw in the bucket and pulled it up once more for Shettu.

SHETTU: *(gasps)* I don't believe it!

WOMAN: Oh, it's not so strange. After all, my husband is Master Man.

BABY: *(makes baby noises)*

NARRATOR 3: When Shettu got home, she told Shadusa what had happened.

SHADUSA: *(furiously)* Master Man?! *He* can't call himself that! *I'm* Master Man. I'll have to teach that fellow a lesson.

SHETTU: *(pleading)* Oh, husband, don't! If the *baby* is so strong, think what the *father* must be like. You'll get yourself killed!

SHADUSA: We'll see about that!

NARRATOR 1: The next morning, Shadusa set out early and walked till he came to the well.

NARRATOR 4: He threw in the bucket—

NARRATOR 1: *SPLASH!*

NARRATOR 4: —then he pulled on the rope. But though he tugged and he heaved, he could not lift the bucket.

NARRATOR 2: Just then the woman with the baby walked up.

BABY: *(makes baby noises)*

SHADUSA: *(to WOMAN, belligerently)* Wait a minute. What do you think you're doing?

WOMAN: I'm getting water, of course.

SHADUSA: Well, you can't. The bucket won't come up.

NARRATOR 3: The woman set down the baby, who quickly pulled up the bucket and filled his mother's calabash.

BABY: *(makes baby noises)*

SHADUSA: Wah! How did he do that?

WOMAN: It's easy—when your father is Master Man.

NARRATOR 1: Shadusa gulped and thought about going home. But instead he thrust out his chest and said,

SHADUSA: I want to meet this fellow, so I can show him who's the *real* Master Man.

WOMAN: Oh, I wouldn't do that. He *devours* men like you! But suit yourself.

BABY: *(makes baby noises)*

NARRATOR 4: So Shadusa followed the woman back to her compound. Inside the fenced yard was a gigantic fireplace, and beside it was a pile of huge bones.

SHADUSA: *(still belligerent)* What's all this?

WOMAN: Well, you see, our hut is so small that my husband must come out here to eat his elephants.

NARRATOR 2: Just then they heard a great

MASTER MAN: *ROAR!*

NARRATOR 2: . . . so loud that Shadusa had to cover his ears. Then the ground began to shake, till Shadusa could hardly stand.

SHADUSA: *(alarmed, shaking with the ground)* What's that?!

WOMAN: *(shaking but calm)* That's Master Man.

SHADUSA: *(still shaking)* Oh, no! You weren't fooling! I've got to get out of here!

WOMAN: *(still shaking)* It's too late now. But let me hide you.

NARRATOR 3: By the fence were some large clay pots, each as tall as a man, for storing grain. She helped him climb into one, then set the lid in place.

NARRATOR 1: Shadusa raised the lid a crack to peek out.

SHADUSA: *(gasps)*

NARRATOR 1: And there coming into the compound was Master Man, carrying a dead elephant across his shoulders.

BABY: *(in delight)* Papa!

WOMAN: *(to MASTER MAN)* Did you have a good day, dear?

MASTER MAN: *(bellowing)* Yes! But I forgot my bow and arrows. I had to kill this elephant with my bare hands.

NARRATOR 4: As Shadusa watched in terror, Master Man built a huge fire in the fireplace, roasted the elephant, and devoured every bit of it but the bones.

NARRATOR 2: Suddenly he stopped and sniffed.

MASTER MAN: *(sniffs loudly)* Wife! I smell a man!

WOMAN: Oh, there's no man here now. One passed by while you were gone. That must be what you smell.

MASTER MAN: Too bad! He would have been tasty.

NARRATOR 3: Then he rolled over on the ground, and before long the leaves trembled from his snores.

NARRATOR 1: The woman hurried over to the pot and slid off the lid.

WOMAN: *(to SHADUSA, in a hushed voice)* Quick! Get away while you can.

NARRATOR 4: Shadusa leaped out and bolted down the path.

NARRATOR 2: But he hadn't gone too far when he heard a distant

MASTER MAN: *(from a distance)* ROAR!

NARRATOR 2: . . . and felt the ground tremble beneath him.

NARRATOR 3: Master Man was coming!

NARRATOR 1: Shadusa ran till he came upon five farmers hoeing a field. One of them called,

FARMER: What's your hurry?

SHADUSA: Master Man is after me!

FARMER: Take it easy. We won't let anyone hurt you.

NARRATOR 4: Just then they heard a terrible

MASTER MAN: *ROAR!*

NARRATOR 2: The farmers all dropped their hoes and covered their ears.

FARMER: What was that?!

SHADUSA: That was Master Man!

FARMER: Well, then, you'd better keep running!

NARRATOR 3: And the five farmers fled across the field.

NARRATOR 1: Shadusa ran on till he met ten porters carrying bundles.

PORTER: *(calling)* What's your hurry?

SHADUSA: Master Man is after me!

PORTER: Relax. No one can fight us all.

NARRATOR 4: Just then the ground quaked, and they all bounced into the air.

NARRATOR 2: The porters fell in a heap, all mixed up with their bundles.

PORTER: What was that?!

SHADUSA: That was Master Man!

PORTER: Then run for your life!

NARRATOR 3: And the ten porters bolted from the path.

NARRATOR 1: Shadusa ran on till he rounded a bend—

NARRATOR 4: then he stopped short.

NARRATOR 2: There beside the path sat a stranger,

NARRATOR 3: and there beside the stranger lay a huge pile of elephant bones.

STRANGER: *(in a growl)* What's your hurry?

SHADUSA: *(in a moan)* Master Man is after me.

STRANGER: You better not say so—'cause *I'm* Master Man!

NARRATOR 1: From behind Shadusa came another

MASTER MAN: *ROAR!*

NARRATOR 1: . . . and once again he bounced into the air.

NARRATOR 4: The stranger caught him in one hand as Master Man ran up.

MASTER MAN: *(to STRANGER, bellowing)* Let me have him!

STRANGER: *(in a growl)* Come and get him!

NARRATOR 2: Master Man lunged, but the stranger tossed Shadusa into a tree. Then the two strong men wrapped themselves around each other and wrestled across the ground.

MASTER MAN: *ROAR!*

STRANGER: *GRRRRR!*

NARRATOR 3: The noise of the battle nearly deafened Shadusa. The dust choked him. The trembling of the tree nearly shook him down.

NARRATOR 1: As Shadusa watched, the two men struggled to their feet, still clutching one another. Then each gave a mighty leap, and together they rose into the air.

NARRATOR 4: Higher and higher they went, till they passed through a cloud and out of sight.

SHADUSA: *(looking up, grows more and more puzzled)*

NARRATOR 2: Shadusa waited and waited, but the men never came back down. At last he climbed carefully from the tree, then ran and ran and never stopped till he got home safe and sound.

NARRATOR 3: And he never called himself Master Man again.

SHADUSA: *(gives loud sigh of relief)*

NARRATOR 1: As for those other two, they're still in the clouds, where they battle on to this day.

NARRATOR 4: Of course, they rest whenever they're both worn out.

NARRATOR 2: But sooner or later they start up again,

NARRATOR 3: and what a noise they make!

MASTER MAN: *ROAR!*

STRANGER: *GRRRRR!*

NARRATOR 1: Some people call that noise thunder.

NARRATOR 4: But now you know what it *really* is—

NARRATOR 2: two fools fighting forever

NARRATOR 3: to see which one is

NARRATORS 1–4: MASTER MAN!

Savitri
A Tale of Ancient India

Told by Aaron Shepard

Adapted for reader's theater by the author, from his picture book published by Albert Whitman, Morton Grove, Illinois, 1992

> For more reader's theater, visit Aaron Shepard's RT Page at
> **www.aaronshep.com/rt**

PREVIEW: The princess Savitri must use all her wit and will to save her husband from the god of death.

GENRE: Myths, folktales, legends
CULTURE: Asian Indian (ancient), Hindu
THEME: Heroines, determination

READERS: 11
READER AGES: 9–15
LENGTH: 10 minutes

ROLES: Narrators 1–3, Savitri, Satyavan, Kings 1 & 2, Teacher, Narada, Yama, Goddess

NOTES: This story is probably around 3000 years old. It was first written down about 2000 years ago as part of the *Mahabharata,* India's great national epic. *Savitri* is pronounced "SAH-vit-ree." *Satyavan* is pronounced "SOT-ya-von." *Narada* is pronounced "NAR-a-da." *Yama* is pronounced "YAH-ma," rhyming with "lama." *Mahabharata* is pronounced "MAH-hah-BAR-a-ta." To hear the names, and for other special features, visit www.aaronshep.com/extras.

NARRATOR 1: In India, in the time of legend, there lived a king with many wives but not one child.

NARRATOR 2: Morning and evening for eighteen years, he faced the fire on the sacred altar and prayed for the gift of children.

NARRATOR 3: Finally, a shining goddess rose from the flames.

GODDESS: I am Savitri, child of the Sun. By your prayers, you have won a daughter.

NARRATOR 1: Within a year, a daughter came to the king and his favorite wife. He named her Savitri, after the goddess.

NARRATOR 2: Beauty and intelligence were the princess Savitri's, and eyes that shone like the sun. So splendid was she, people thought she herself was a goddess.

NARRATOR 3: Yet when the time came for her to marry, no man asked for her. Her father told her,

KING 1: Weak men turn away from radiance like yours. Go out and find a man worthy of you. Then I will arrange the marriage.

NARRATOR 1: In the company of servants and councilors, Savitri traveled from place to place.

NARRATOR 2: After many days, she came upon a hermitage by a river crossing. Here lived many who had left the towns and cities for a life of prayer and study.

NARRATOR 3: Savitri entered the hall of worship and bowed to the eldest teacher. As they spoke, a young man with shining eyes came into the hall. He guided another man, old and blind.

SAVITRI: *(softly, to the teacher)* Who is that young man?

TEACHER: *(smiling)* That is Prince Satyavan. He guides his father, a king whose realm was conquered. It is well that Satyavan's name means "Son of Truth," for no man is richer in virtue.

NARRATOR 1: When Savitri returned home, she found her father with the holy seer called Narada.

KING 1: Daughter, have you found a man you wish to marry?

SAVITRI: Yes, father. His name is Satyavan.

NARADA: *(gasps)* Not Satyavan! Princess, no man could be more worthy, but you must not marry him! I know the future. Satyavan will die, one year from today!

KING 1: Do you hear, daughter? Choose a different husband!

NARRATOR 2: Savitri trembled but said,

SAVITRI: I have chosen Satyavan, and I will not choose another. However long or short his life, I wish to share it.

NARRATOR 3: Soon the king went with Savitri to arrange the marriage.

NARRATOR 1: Satyavan was overjoyed to be offered such a bride. But his father, the blind king, asked Savitri,

KING 2: Can you bear the hard life of the hermitage? Will you wear our simple robe, and our coat of matted bark? Will you eat only fruit and plants of the wild?

SAVITRI: I care nothing about comfort or hardship. In palace or in hermitage, I am content.

NARRATOR 2: That very day, Savitri and Satyavan walked hand in hand around the sacred fire in the hall of worship.

NARRATOR 3: In front of all the priests and hermits, they became husband and wife.

* * *

NARRATOR 1: For a year, they lived happily. But Savitri could never forget that Satyavan's death drew closer.

NARRATOR 2: Finally, only three days remained. Savitri entered the hall of worship and faced the sacred fire. There she prayed for three days and nights, not eating or sleeping.

SATYAVAN: My love, prayer and fasting are good. But why be this hard on yourself?

NARRATOR 3: Savitri gave no answer.

NARRATOR 1: The sun was just rising when Savitri at last left the hall. She saw Satyavan heading for the forest, an ax on his shoulder.

NARRATOR 2: Savitri rushed to his side.

SAVITRI: I will come with you.

SATYAVAN: Stay here, my love. You should eat and rest.

SAVITRI: My heart is set on going.

NARRATOR 3: Hand in hand, Savitri and Satyavan walked over wooded hills. They smelled the blossoms on flowering trees, and paused beside clear streams. The cries of peacocks echoed through the woods.

NARRATOR 1: While Savitri rested, Satyavan chopped firewood from a fallen tree. Suddenly, he dropped his ax.

SATYAVAN: My head aches.

NARRATOR 2: Savitri rushed to him. She set him down in the shade of a tree.

SATYAVAN: My body is burning! What is wrong with me?

NARRATOR 3: Satyavan's eyes closed. His breathing slowed.

NARRATOR 1: Savitri looked up.

NARRATOR 2: Coming through the woods to meet them was a princely man. He shone, though his skin was darker than the darkest night. His eyes and his robe were the red of blood.

NARRATOR 3: Trembling, Savitri asked,

SAVITRI: Who *are* you?

YAMA: *(gently)* Princess, you see me only by the power of your prayer and fasting. I am Yama, god of death. Now is the time I must take the spirit of Satyavan.

NARRATOR 1: Yama took a small noose and passed it through Satyavan's breast, as if through air. He drew out a tiny likeness of Satyavan, no bigger than a thumb. Satyavan's breathing stopped.

YAMA: Happiness awaits your husband in my kingdom. Satyavan is a man of great virtue.

NARRATOR 2: Yama placed the likeness inside his robe. Then he turned and headed south, back to his domain.

NARRATOR 3: Savitri rose and started after him.

NARRATOR 1: Yama strode smoothly and swiftly through the woods, while Savitri struggled to keep up. Finally, Yama turned to face her.

YAMA: Savitri! You cannot follow to the land of the dead!

SAVITRI: Lord Yama, I know your duty is to take my husband. But my duty as his wife is to stay beside him!

YAMA: Princess, that duty is at an end! Still, I admire your loyalty. I will grant you a favor—anything but the life of your husband.

SAVITRI: Please restore my father-in-law's kingdom and his sight.

YAMA: His sight and his kingdom shall be restored.

NARRATOR 2: Yama again headed south.

NARRATOR 3: Savitri followed.

NARRATOR 1: Along a riverbank, thorns and tall sharp grass let Yama pass untouched. But they tore at Savitri's clothes and skin.

YAMA: Savitri! You have come far enough!

SAVITRI: Lord Yama, I know my husband will find happiness in your kingdom. But you carry away the happiness that is mine!

YAMA: Princess, even love must bend to fate! Still, I admire your devotion. I will grant you another favor—anything but the life of your husband.

SAVITRI: Grant many more children to my father.

YAMA: Your father shall have many more children.

NARRATOR 2: Yama once more turned south.

NARRATOR 3: Again, Savitri followed.

NARRATOR 1: Up a steep hill Yama glided, while Savitri clambered after. At the top, Yama halted.

YAMA: Savitri! I forbid you to come farther!

SAVITRI: Lord Yama, you are respected and revered by all. Yet no matter what may come, I will remain by Satyavan!

YAMA: Princess, I tell you for the last time, you will not! Still, I can only admire your courage and your firmness. I will grant you one last favor—*anything* but the life of your husband!

SAVITRI: Then grant many children to *me*. And let them be children of Satyavan!

NARRATOR 2: Yama's eyes grew wide as he stared at Savitri.

YAMA: You did not ask for your husband's life, yet I cannot grant your wish without releasing him. Princess! Your wit is as strong as your will.

NARRATOR 3: Yama took out the spirit of Satyavan and removed the noose. The spirit flew north, quickly vanishing from sight.

YAMA: Return, Savitri. You have won your husband's life. *(leaves)*

NARRATOR 1: The sun was just setting when Savitri made her way back to Satyavan.

NARRATOR 2: His chest rose and fell.

NARRATOR 3: His eyes opened.

SATYAVAN: Is the day already gone? I have slept long. But what is wrong, my love? You smile and cry at the same time!

SAVITRI: My love, let us return home.

* * *

NARRATOR 1: Yama was true to all he had promised.

NARRATOR 2: Savitri's father became father to many more.

NARRATOR 3: Satyavan's father regained both sight and kingdom.

NARRATOR 1: In time, Satyavan became king, and Savitri his queen.

NARRATOR 2: They lived long and happily, blessed with many children.

NARRATOR 3: So they had no fear or tears when Yama came again to carry them to his kingdom.

The Enchanted Storks
A Tale of Bagdad

Told by Aaron Shepard

Adapted for reader's theater by the author, from his picture book published by Clarion, New York, 1995

For more reader's theater, visit Aaron Shepard's RT Page at
www.aaronshep.com/rt

PREVIEW: The Calif and his Vizier try a spell that changes them into storks, then find they can't change back.

GENRE: Fairy tales, folktales
CULTURE: Iraqi, Middle Eastern
THEME: Recklessness

READERS: 13 or more
READER AGES: 10–15
LENGTH: 14 minutes

ROLES: Narrators 1–4, Calif, Vizier, Khadur, Omar, Princess, Magicians (4), (Guards)

NOTES: This story began as an original fairy tale by the 19th-century German author Wilhelm Hauff in his book *The Caravan*—but it was so popular that it came to be told by storytellers in the Middle East itself. This retelling is based on both original and retold versions. For best effect, place NARRATORS 1 and 2 at far left, and 3 and 4 at far right, as seen from the audience. To reduce the number of roles, the NARRATORS can double as the MAGICIANS. *Calif* is pronounced "KAY-lif." *Vizier,* a prime minister, is pronounced "viz-EER." *Casalavair* is pronounced "ka-SAH-lah-VAIR." *Omar* is pronounced "O-mar." *Khadur* is pronounced "kah-DOOR," rhyming with "tour." *Allah,* the Arabic word for "God," is pronounced "AH-LAH." To hear the names, and for other special features, visit www.aaronshep.com/extras.

NARRATOR 1: If favor

NARRATOR 2: now

NARRATOR 3: should greet

NARRATOR 4: our story,

NARRATOR 1: Allah

NARRATOR 2: must

NARRATOR 3: receive

NARRATOR 4: the glory.

NARRATOR 1: Once, in the great and glorious city of Bagdad, there was a Calif—Commander of the Faithful and ruler of all Islam.

NARRATOR 4: The people of Bagdad loved their ruler, yet one thing mystified them. All who came before him were amazed by his intimate knowledge of their daily lives.

NARRATOR 2: "The Calif has a thousand eyes," muttered some, glancing behind them for spies. But the Calif's real secret was this:

NARRATOR 3: Each afternoon, he and his trusted Vizier, Ali ben Manzar, would disguise themselves as merchants and slip through a hidden door in the palace wall. Then they would roam the bazaars of the city, listening to the talk and gossip of the day.

NARRATOR 1: One afternoon, as the Calif and his Vizier made their way through the market, an old and wizened man thrust one of his wares under the Calif's nose.

CALIF: What a lovely snuffbox! Look, Ali ben Manzar. See the intricate carving and jeweled inlay. Peddler, what will you ask for it?

KHADUR: *(wheezing)* Just one gold coin.

NARRATOR 4: The Calif gave him two, took the box, and walked on.

NARRATOR 2: Reaching the edge of the city, the Calif and his Vizier strolled through the parks and orchards beyond.

NARRATOR 3: At last they stopped to rest by a quiet lake.

CALIF: I wonder if my new box holds any snuff.

NARRATOR 1: The Calif opened the tiny box and found it filled with the pungent powder.

CALIF: But what is this?

NARRATOR 4: He pulled a piece of parchment from the underside of the lid.

NARRATOR 2: The Vizier craned his neck to see.

VIZIER: What does it say, Glorious Lord?

CALIF: *(reading)*

> A sniff of snuff, for wings to soar.
> *Casalavair* for hands once more.

> *(to VIZIER)* Why, I believe the snuff is magic!

NARRATOR 3: He looked longingly at the sky.

CALIF: I have always wanted to see my city from the air.

VIZIER: Perhaps we should be cautious. What if the charm fails to change us back?

CALIF: If the snuff works, then surely the magic word will too. Come, let us try our luck!

NARRATOR 1: He held out the box, and each took a pinch of snuff. Then together they inhaled the powder.

NARRATOR 4: A flurry of wings, beaks, and feathers—and there in place of the Calif and his Vizier stood two storks.

CALIF: Wonderful!

NARRATOR 2: . . . the Calif said, snapping and clattering his beak—for that is how storks talk.

NARRATOR 3: A human would have heard only

CALIF: *Calap! Calap!*

NARRATOR 3: But since both the Calif and his Vizier were now birds, Ali ben Manzar understood perfectly.

VIZIER: *Calap! Calap!* Quite amazing!

CALIF: *Calap! Calap!* Let us test our wings!

NARRATOR 1: The two storks rose into the air, circling higher and higher. Spread below were meadows, ornamental gardens, orchards, and fields of crops.

NARRATOR 4: The great river Tigris flowed slowly across the plain, sprouting canals along its length. And basking on the banks of the river was Bagdad, capital of all Islam, City of Peace.

CALIF: *(calling to VIZIER)* Breathtaking, is it not? Come, let us fly over the city.

NARRATOR 2: Soon they soared above the streets, canals, bridges, and clay-brick buildings of Bagdad.

NARRATOR 3: In courtyard and bazaar, people bought and sold, worked and rested, fought and prayed, stole and chased, kissed and parted, laughed and wept.

CALIF: Truly, a stork knows more of this city than the Calif himself.

NARRATOR 1: As evening drew near, the Vizier called,

VIZIER: Glorious Lord, we had best return to the palace.

NARRATOR 4: Back they flew to the lake and landed by the snuffbox. The Calif once more read the parchment, then cried,

CALIF: Casalavair!

NARRATOR 2: And there stood—two storks.

CALIF: *(in alarm)* Casalavair! *(growing desperate)* Casalavair! Casalavair!

NARRATOR 3: But storks they remained.

CALIF: *(terrified)* Ali ben Manzar, you try it!

VIZIER: *(equally terrified)* Casalavair! Casalavair!

CALIF & VIZIER: *(keep repeating beneath NARRATOR, below; not in unison)* Casalavair! Casalavair!

NARRATOR 1: *(over CALIF and VIZIER, above)* But no matter how they called and hopped and flapped their wings, nothing changed.

NARRATOR 4: At last they stood exhausted.

VIZIER: It seems some enemy has lured us into this enchantment.

CALIF: But what can we do?

VIZIER: I know of nothing. Without the proper word to break the spell, we may never regain our true forms.

NARRATOR 2: The sun dipped into the lake as the two storks stood lost in thought. Finally the Calif said,

CALIF: Stork or not, my stomach aches for food. What are we to eat?

VIZIER: Why, Glorious Lord, we must eat what every stork eats! Fish and mice, frogs and toads, snakes and eels, snails and slugs, worms and grubs.

NARRATOR 3: So the storks poked their beaks among rushes at the lake edge and into holes along the bank. When they had eaten as much as they could bear, each stood on one leg, crossed the other leg against it, hid his beak among his breast feathers, and slept.

* * *

NARRATOR 1: The next morning, they hid the snuffbox and flew to the palace. From high on a turret they watched the frantic scene within the palace walls. Soldiers, courtiers, and servants rushed about in search of the Calif and the Vizier—a search the storks knew too well was in vain.

VIZIER: *(looking the other way)* Look, Glorious Lord! A caravan approaches!

NARRATOR 4: Through the streets of Bagdad came a magnificent procession of horsemen, camel riders, and servants on foot. At its head rode a horseman in regal dress.

CALIF: By the beard of the Prophet! It is my brother Omar! He has long coveted my throne.

NARRATOR 2: The caravan reached the gate, and the horseman called to the guards.

OMAR: I am Omar, brother to the Calif. I have learned by secret means that the Calif is missing and will not return. As true successor of the Prophet Mohammed, I have come to take my brother's place as Commander of the Faithful, ruler of all Islam.

CALIF: *(to the guards)* Do not open the gate!

NARRATOR 3: But all that was heard from the Calif by the startled people below was

CALIF: *Calap! Calap! (keep repeating beneath NARRATOR, below)*

NARRATOR 3: *(over CALIF, above)* And when they looked up, all they saw was two storks—one of them hopping madly, flapping its wings, and clattering its beak.

OMAR: *(to the guards)* You see? Even the storks welcome me. Open the gate!

NARRATOR 1: The gate opened, and Omar rode through in triumph.

NARRATOR 4: High on the turret, the Calif stood silent and still.

VIZIER: *(gently)* Glorious Lord, we can do nothing here. Let us fly far from the city. In solitude we may find the strength to bear our fate.

NARRATOR 2: The two soared away, beyond the city and the plains, to a lonely forest in the foothills of the great mountains.

NARRATOR 3: There they began their new life. They dined on tree toads and fish, and tried not to speak of Bagdad or the affairs of a Calif.

NARRATOR 1: One afternoon, the storks wandered into a different part of the forest.

VIZIER: How gloomy and silent it is here. Not even a rustle of leaves.

NARRATOR 4: Just then, a quick *tap-tap-tap* made them jump. They turned to see a woodpecker hunting for worms in the bark of a tree.

NARRATOR 2: To their amazement, tears flowed from the woodpecker's eyes.

CALIF: Good woodpecker, why do you weep?

PRINCESS: *(through her tears)* Why should I not? You were born a bird and have known no other life, but I am a princess. The evil sorcerer Khadur threw this spell upon me, for I would not marry him. And a bird I must remain till another man asks me to wed. *(sniffs)* Imagine, a man proposing to a bird! Do you see now why I weep?

CALIF: *(thoughtfully)* I do. But how did you come to this forest? Is the sorcerer himself hereabouts?

NARRATOR 3: The woodpecker pointed with her beak.

PRINCESS: There is a clearing nearby. He meets there every night with his magicians.

CALIF: *(aside to VIZIER)* Come, Ali ben Manzar. We may find a way to help our little friend—and perhaps ourselves as well.

NARRATOR 1: Making their way through the thick forest, the Calif and his Vizier reached a wide, rocky circle where no plant grew.

NARRATOR 4: They hid themselves in the bushes at its edge and waited for the gathering dark.

NARRATOR 2: As the moon rose and cast its light into the clearing, four cloaked men entered the circle by different paths. They built a fire on a tall, flat rock in the very center and sat cross-legged around it.

NARRATOR 3: Then the flames leaped, and a fifth cloaked figure stood among them. The magicians touched their heads to the ground.

MAGICIANS: Hail, Khadur, greatest of sorcerers!

CALIF: *(gasps)* By the beard of the Prophet! It is the peddler who sold us the box!

NARRATOR 1: Before the storks could recover from this surprise, there was another. With a clatter of hooves, into the clearing rode the Calif's brother, Omar!

OMAR: Greetings, sorcerer.

KHADUR: *(wheezing)* Greetings, Glorious Lord. And how do you fare in the city of Bagdad?

OMAR: Excellently. The people long for their old ruler, but they learn to fear me and obey. As for you, sorcerer, you have well earned your reward.

NARRATOR 4: He threw Khadur a bulging pouch, which clinked as the sorcerer caught it.

OMAR: But you have not yet told me—how did you get rid of my brother?

KHADUR: *(wheezes with laughter)* Nothing easier, Glorious Lord. I disguised myself as a peddler and sold him a box of magic snuff. Your brother and his dolt of a Vizier changed themselves most obligingly into storks! I even provided the word of disenchantment—or nearly so.

OMAR: What do you mean?

KHADUR: I switched two letters. I wrote *Casalavair* instead of *Calasavair.* *(wheezes with laughter)*

NARRATOR 2: The sorcerer laughed till he choked.

OMAR: A true master! I will have need of your services again.

NARRATOR 3: He spurred his horse and raced from the clearing.

KHADUR: *(to MAGICIANS)* Now, to work! We have spells to prepare.

CALIF: There will be no spells tonight!

NARRATOR 1: All that the men heard was

CALIF: *Calap! Calap!*

NARRATOR 1: . . . but two storks were suddenly upon them, pummeling them with strong wings, pecking them with sharp beaks.

KHADUR: It's the Calif and the Vizier!

NARRATOR 4: Khadur fled from the clearing, his magicians close behind.

VIZIER: Should we not follow, Glorious Lord?

CALIF: No, Ali ben Manzar. We have spells to undo.

NARRATOR 2: Even as he spoke, the woodpecker alighted beside them.

PRINCESS: *(anxiously)* What was that noise?

CALIF: You shall know presently, dear Princess.

NARRATOR 3: Then drawing an anxious breath, he cried,

CALIF: Calasavair!

NARRATOR 1: A flurry of wings, beaks, and feathers—and there in place of two storks stood the Calif and his Vizier.

NARRATOR 4: The Calif turned to the astonished woodpecker.

CALIF: Princess, will you honor me by becoming my wife?

NARRATOR 2: Another flurry of feathers,

NARRATOR 3: and there stood a young woman of slender figure and dancing eyes.

PRINCESS: *(smiling shyly)* The honor will be mine. *(offers CALIF her hand)*

CALIF: *(takes it happily)*

* * *

NARRATOR 1: The next day, they borrowed horses at a nearby village and rode into Bagdad. By the time they reached the palace, a joyous crowd had gathered behind them.

CALIF: *(to the guards)* Open the gate!

NARRATOR 4: The gate flew open just as Omar appeared in the palace yard.

NARRATOR 2: When Omar saw the Calif, he turned the color of parchment.

CALIF: *(to the guards)* Seize him!

NARRATOR 3: The guards dragged Omar before the Calif.

OMAR: *(pleading)* Brother, spare my life!

CALIF: For your treason, I should behead you. But instead I will banish you by ship to the farthest end of the earth. And by the beard of the Prophet, on the voyage you will eat nothing but toads and snails!

* * *

NARRATOR 1: And so the Calif regained his throne, and gained a lovely wife besides.

NARRATOR 4: And if he seemed to know even more about his people than before, no one guessed how.

NARRATOR 2: How would they?

NARRATOR 3: For few even noticed the pair of storks that soared on many an afternoon above the streets of Bagdad.

NARRATOR 1: The Calif

NARRATOR 2: saw

NARRATOR 3: much more

NARRATOR 4: than we,

NARRATOR 1: but how much

NARRATOR 2: more

NARRATOR 3: does Allah

NARRATOR 4: see.

The Crystal Heart
A Vietnamese Legend

Told by Aaron Shepard

Adapted for reader's theater by the author, from his picture book published by Atheneum, New York, 1998

> For more reader's theater, visit Aaron Shepard's RT Page at
> **www.aaronshep.com/rt**

PREVIEW: The mandarin's daughter did not really see the boatman who sang from the river, but she's sure he's her destined love.

GENRE: Folktales
CULTURE: Vietnamese
THEME: Kindness, false imagining

READERS: 13
READER AGES: 10 and up
LENGTH: 10 minutes

ROLES: Narrators 1–3, Mi Nuong, Truong Chi, Maid, Mandarin, Doctor, Messenger, Villagers 1–4

NOTES: MAID, MANDARIN, DOCTOR, and MESSENGER can double as VILLAGERS. *Mi Nuong* is pronounced "MEEN WONG." *Truong Chi* is pronounced "troo-ONG CHEE." Below is the tune for "The Song of the Fisherman," an original composition of the author's. To hear the names and the music, and for other special features, visit www.aaronshep.com/extras.

NARRATOR 1: Long ago, in a palace by the Red River, there lived a great mandarin and his daughter, Mi Nuong.

NARRATOR 2: Like other young ladies of her position, Mi Nuong was kept indoors, away from the eyes of admiring men. She spent most of her time in her room at the top of a tower.

NARRATOR 3: There she would sit on a bench by a moon-shaped window, reading or embroidering, chatting with her maid, and gazing out often at the garden and the river.

NARRATOR 1: One day as she sat there, a song floated to her from the distance, in a voice deep and sweet. She looked out and saw a fishing boat coming up the river. She asked her maid,

MI NUONG: Do you hear it? How beautifully he sings!

NARRATOR 2: She listened again as the voice drew nearer.

TRUONG CHI: *(singing in the distance)*

>   My love is like a blossom in the breeze.
>   My love is like a moonbeam on the waves.

MI NUONG: He must be young and very handsome. *(with a sudden thrill)* Perhaps he knows I am here and sings it just for me!

NARRATOR 3: The maid's eyes lit up.

MAID: My lady, perhaps he's a mandarin's son in disguise—the man you are destined to marry!

NARRATOR 1: Mi Nuong felt a flush on her face and a stirring in her heart.

NARRATOR 2: She tried to make out the man's features, but he was too far off to see clearly.

NARRATOR 3: The boat and the song glided slowly up the river and away.

MI NUONG: *(softly)* Yes. Perhaps he is.

NARRATOR 1: All day long, Mi Nuong waited by the window, hoping to hear the singer again.

NARRATOR 2: The next day she waited too, and the next.

NARRATOR 3: But the voice did not return.

MI NUONG: *(sadly, to MAID)* Why doesn't he come?

NARRATOR 1: As the days passed, Mi Nuong grew pale and weak. At last she went to her bed and stayed there.

NARRATOR 2: The mandarin came to her.

MANDARIN: Daughter, what's wrong?

MI NUONG: *(faintly)* It's nothing, Father.

NARRATOR 3: The mandarin sent for the doctor. But after seeing Mi Nuong, the doctor told him,

DOCTOR: I can find no illness. And without an illness, I can offer no cure.

NARRATOR 1: The weeks passed, and Mi Nuong grew no better.

NARRATOR 2: Then one day her maid came before the mandarin.

MAID: My lord, I know what ails your daughter. Mi Nuong is sick for love. To cure her, you must find the handsome young man who sings these words. *(recites)*

> My love is like a blossom in the breeze.
> My love is like a moonbeam on the waves.

MANDARIN: It will be done.

NARRATOR 3: And he sent out a messenger at once.

NARRATOR 1: Days later, the messenger returned.

MESSENGER: *(bowing)* Lord, in no great house of this province does any young man know the song. But I found in a nearby village a man who sings it, a fisherman named Truong Chi. I have brought him to the palace.

MANDARIN: *(in disbelief)* A fisherman? Let me see him.

NARRATOR 2: The messenger brought him in.

NARRATOR 3: The fisherman stood uneasily, his eyes wide as they cast about the richly furnished room.

NARRATOR 1: For a moment, the mandarin was too astounded to speak. The man was neither young nor handsome. His clothes were ragged and he stank of fish.

NARRATOR 2: "Certainly no match for my daughter!" thought the mandarin. "Somehow, she must not realize . . . ."

NARRATOR 3: He gave his order to the messenger.

MANDARIN: Bring the fisherman to my daughter's door and have him sing his song.

NARRATOR 1: Soon Truong Chi stood anxiously outside the young lady's room. He could not understand why they'd brought him here.

NARRATOR 2: What could they want? He was just a fisherman, wishing only to make an honest living. He had hurt no one, done nothing wrong!

NARRATOR 3: At the messenger's signal, he nervously started to sing.

TRUONG CHI: *(singing)*

> My love is like a blossom in the breeze.
> My love is like a moonbeam on the waves.

NARRATOR 1: In the room beyond the door, Mi Nuong's eyes flew open.

MI NUONG: *(to MAID)* He's here! How can that be? Oh, quickly, help me dress!

NARRATOR 2: Mi Nuong jumped from her bed. Never had she so swiftly clothed herself, put up her hair, made herself up. By the time the song drew to a close, she looked like a heavenly vision in flowing robes.

MI NUONG: Now, open the door!

NARRATOR 3: Mi Nuong tried to calm her wildly beating heart. She forced herself to stand shyly, casting her eyes down in the manner proper to a modest young lady.

NARRATOR 1: As the door pulled open, Truong Chi shrank back, not knowing what to expect.

NARRATOR 2: Then all at once he found himself gazing on the greatest beauty he had ever known.

NARRATOR 3: He felt his heart leap, and in that moment, he fell deeply, hopelessly, desperately in love.

NARRATOR 1: Mi Nuong could not wait a moment longer.

NARRATOR 2: She lifted her eyes to look upon her beloved.

NARRATOR 3: And in that moment, her eyes grew wide and she burst out laughing.

MI NUONG: *(laughs in astonishment)*

NARRATOR 1: A mandarin's son? Her destined love?

NARRATOR 2: Why, he was nothing but a common fisherman! How terribly, terribly silly she'd been!

NARRATOR 3: Shaking with mirth at her folly, she turned her head away and whispered,

MI NUONG: *(whispering to MAID)* Close the door.

NARRATOR 1: The door shut in Truong Chi's face. He stood there frozen, the young lady's laughter ringing in his ears. He felt his heart grow cold and hard.

NARRATOR 2: Truong Chi was sent home. But he could not go on as before. Hardly eating or sleeping, he grew pale and ill. He no longer cared if he lived or died.

NARRATOR 3: And so, he died.

NARRATOR 1: The villagers found him on the sleeping mat in his hut. On his chest sat a large crystal.

VILLAGER 1: What is it?

VILLAGER 2: It is his heart. The laugh of the mandarin's daughter wounded it so deeply, it turned hard to stop the pain.

VILLAGER 3: What do we do with it? It is very lovely. Like one of his songs!

VILLAGER 4: We should put it in his boat, and let it float down to the sea.

NARRATOR 2: At sundown, they set the crystal in the fisherman's boat.

NARRATOR 3: Then they pushed the boat from its mooring and watched in sorrow as it drifted down the river and out of sight.

NARRATOR 1: But the boat did not drift to the sea.

NARRATOR 2: It came to shore by the mandarin's palace.

NARRATOR 3: And so it was that the mandarin found it at sunrise as he strolled along the bank.

MANDARIN: What have we here?

NARRATOR 1: The mandarin reached in to pick up the crystal. He turned it over in his hand, examining and admiring it.

MANDARIN: What a splendid gift the river has brought!

NARRATOR 2: A few days later, when no one had claimed it, the mandarin sent it to a turner to be made into a teacup.

NARRATOR 3: He brought the cup one evening to Mi Nuong's room.

MANDARIN: *(to MI NUONG, handing it to her)* A gift for my lovely daughter.

MI NUONG: Oh, Father, it's beautiful! I can hardly wait to drink from it!

NARRATOR 1: When the mandarin left, she told her maid,

MI NUONG: It's late, so you can go to bed. But first make me some tea, so I can drink from my cup.

NARRATOR 2: The maid finished her task and went off. Mi Nuong poured the tea, blew out the candles on the table, and carried the cup to her window seat.

NARRATOR 3: A full moon shone into the room, and looking out, she watched the moonlight play upon the river. The scent of blossoms drifted from the garden.

NARRATOR 1: Mi Nuong lifted the cup to her lips.

NARRATOR 2: But just as she was about to drink . . .

MI NUONG: *(in surprise and fear, staring into cup)* Oh!

NARRATOR 3: She quickly set the cup down on the bench.

NARRATOR 1: On the surface of the tea was the face of Truong Chi, gazing at her with eyes filled with love.

NARRATOR 2: And now his sweet song filled the room, familiar but a little changed.

TRUONG CHI: *(singing)*

>   Mi Nuong is like a blossom in the breeze.
>   Mi Nuong is like a moonbeam on the waves.

NARRATOR 3: And Mi Nuong remembered those eyes she had seen so briefly through the open door, and she remembered her laugh.

MI NUONG: What have I done? I was so cruel! I didn't mean to hurt you. I didn't know. . . . I'm sorry. So very, very sorry!

NARRATOR 1: Her eyes filled with tears. A single tear dropped into the cup.

NARRATOR 2: It was enough. The crystal melted away, releasing the spirit of Truong Chi.

NARRATOR 3: Then Mi Nuong heard the song one last time, floating off over the river.

TRUONG CHI: *(singing in the distance)*

  Mi Nuong is like a blossom in the breeze.
  Mi Nuong is like a moonbeam on the waves.

MI NUONG: *(softly)* Good-bye. . . . Good-bye.

* * *

NARRATOR 1: It was not many months more when Mi Nuong was given in marriage to the son of a great mandarin.

NARRATOR 2: He was young and handsome, and she felt that her dreams had come true.

NARRATOR 3: Yet now, as she gazed on a different garden and a different view of the river, she often still heard the song of the fisherman echo softly in her heart.

The Sea King's Daughter
A Russian Legend

Told by Aaron Shepard

Adapted for reader's theater by the author, from his picture book published by Atheneum, New York, 1997

For more reader's theater, visit Aaron Shepard's RT Page at
www.aaronshep.com/rt

PREVIEW: A poor musician is invited to play in the Sea King's palace, where he's offered more than riches.

GENRE: Legends, folktales, epic ballads
CULTURE: Russian (medieval)
THEME: Making choices; value of arts

READERS: 9 or more
READER AGES: 10 and up
LENGTH: 10 minutes

ROLES: Narrators 1 & 2, Sadko, Sea King, Sea Queen, Volkhova, Host, Friend, Captain, (Merchant), (Dancers)

NOTES: This is a retelling of the most popular of Russia's epic ballads, the legend of the merchant-musician Sadko. It takes place in Novgorod, the greatest commercial center of medieval Russia. For best effect, place NARRATOR 1 at far left, and NARRATOR 2 at far right, as seen from the audience. *Novgorod* is pronounced "NOV-go-rod." *Sadko* is pronounced "SOD-ko," rhyming with "sod go." *Gusli*, a type of psaltery, is pronounced "GOOSS-lee," sounding like "goose lee." *Volkhov* sounds like "vole cove." *Volkhova* is pronounced "VOLE-ko-vah," sounding like "vole cove ah." Performance of this script can be enhanced by recorded music as called for. Though the Russian gusli is recorded mostly as part of balalaika orchestras, the Finnish kantele is a close cousin and is commonly recorded on its own. Kantele resources are easily found by searching the Web. To hear the names, and for other special features, visit www.aaronshep.com/extras.

NARRATOR 1: Long ago, in the river port city called Novgorod the Great, there lived a young musician named Sadko.

NARRATOR 2: Every day, a rich merchant or noble would send a messenger to Sadko's door, calling him to play at a feast. Sadko would grab his twelve-string *gusli* and rush to the banquet hall. There he'd pluck the strings of his instrument till all the guests were dancing.

HOST: Eat your fill!

NARRATOR 1: . . . the host would tell him later, pointing him to the table, and passing him a few small coins besides.

NARRATOR 2: And on such as he was given did Sadko live.

NARRATOR 1: Often his friends would ask him,

FRIEND: How can you survive on so little?

SADKO: It's not so bad.

NARRATOR 2: . . . Sadko would reply.

SADKO: And anyway, how many men can go to a different feast each day, play the music they love, and watch it set a whole room dancing?

NARRATOR 1: Sadko was proud of his city, the richest and most free in all Russia. He would walk through busy Market Square, lined with merchants in their stalls and teeming with traders from many lands. He never crossed the square without hearing tongues of far-off places, from Italy to Norway to Persia.

NARRATOR 2: Down at the piers, he would see the sailing ships with their cargos of lumber, grain, hides, pottery, spices, and precious metals. And crossing the Great Bridge over the River Volkhov, Sadko would catch the glint from the gilded roofs of a dozen white stone churches.

SADKO: Is there another such city as Novgorod in all the world? Is there any better place to be?

NARRATOR 1: Yet sometimes Sadko was lonely.

NARRATOR 2: The maidens who danced gaily to his music at the feasts would often smile at him, and more than one had set his heart on fire. But they were rich and he was poor, and not one of them would think of being his.

NARRATOR 1: One lonely evening, Sadko walked sadly beyond the city walls and down along the broad River Volkhov. He came to his favorite spot on the bank and set his gusli on his lap.

NARRATOR 2: Gentle waves brushed the shore, and moonlight shimmered on the water.

SADKO: *(sighs)* My lovely River Volkhov. Rich man, poor man—it's all the same to you. If only you were a woman! I'd marry you and live with you here in the city I love.

NARRATOR 1: Sadko plucked a sad tune, then a peaceful one, then a merry one. The tinkling notes of his gusli floated over the Volkhov.

NARRATOR 2: All at once the river grew rough, and strong waves began to slap the bank.

SADKO: Heaven help me!

NARRATOR 1: . . . cried Sadko as a large shape rose from the water.

NARRATOR 2: Before him stood a huge man, with a pearl-encrusted crown atop a flowing mane of seaweed.

SEA KING: Musician, behold the King of the Sea. To this river I have come to visit one of my daughters, the Princess Volkhova. Your sweet music reached us on the river bottom, where it pleased us greatly.

SADKO: *(stammering a little)* Thank you, Your Majesty.

SEA KING: Soon I will return to my own palace. I wish you to play there at a feast.

SADKO: Gladly. But where is it? And how do I get there?

SEA KING: Why, under the sea, of course! I'm sure you'll find your way. But meanwhile, you need not wait for your reward.

NARRATOR 1: Something large jumped from the river and flopped at Sadko's feet. A fish with golden scales! As Sadko watched in amazement, it stiffened and turned to solid gold.

SADKO: Your Majesty, you are too generous!

SEA KING: Say no more about it! Music is worth far more than gold. If the world were fair, you'd have your fill of riches!

NARRATOR 2: And with a splash, he sank in the river and was gone.

* * *

NARRATOR 1: The next morning, Sadko arrived at the market square just as the stalls were opening. He quickly sold the golden fish to an astonished merchant. Then, hurrying to the piers, he booked his passage on a ship leaving Novgorod that very day.

NARRATOR 2: Down the Volkhov the ship sailed, across Lake Ladoga and the Gulf of Finland, and into the Baltic Sea. As it sped above the deep water, Sadko peered over the rail.

SADKO: *(softly, to himself)* In all the wide sea, how can I ever find the palace?

NARRATOR 1: Just then, the ship shuddered to a halt. The wind filled the sails, yet the ship stood still, as if a giant hand had grasped it. The captain cried out to his crew,

CAPTAIN: It must be the King of the Sea! Perhaps he seeks tribute— or someone among us.

SADKO: Do not be troubled. I know the one he seeks.

NARRATOR 2: And, clutching his gusli, he jumped from the ship.

NARRATOR 1: Down sank Sadko, down all the way to the sea floor. The red sun shone dimly through the water above, while before him stood a white stone palace.

NARRATOR 2: Sadko passed through a coral gate. As he reached the huge palace doors, they swung open to reveal a giant hall.

NARRATOR 1: The elegant room was filled with guests and royal attendants—herring and sprats, cod and flounder, gobies and sticklebacks, sand eels and sea scorpions, crabs and lobsters, starfish and squid, sea turtles and giant sturgeon.

NARRATOR 2: Standing among the guests were dozens of maidens— river nymphs, the Sea King's daughters. On a shell throne at the end of the hall sat the Sea King and his Queen.

SEA KING: You're just in time! Musician, come sit by me—and let the dance begin!

NARRATOR 1: Sadko set his gusli on his lap and plucked a merry tune. Soon all the fish swam in graceful figures. The seafloor crawlers cavorted. The river maidens leaped and spun.

SEA KING: I like that tune!

NARRATOR 2: The King jumped to the center of the hall and joined the dance. His arms waved, his robe swirled, his hair streamed, his feet stamped.

SEA KING: Faster! Play faster!

NARRATOR 1: Sadko played faster and the King's dance grew wilder. All the others stopped and watched in awe. Ever more madly did he move, whirling faster, leaping higher, stamping harder.

NARRATOR 2: The Sea Queen whispered urgently,

SEA QUEEN: Musician, end your tune! It seems to you the King merely dances in his hall. But above us, the sea is tossing ships like toys, and giant waves are breaking on the shore!

NARRATOR 1: Alarmed, Sadko pulled a string till it snapped.

SADKO: Your Majesty, my gusli is broken.

SEA KING: A shame.

NARRATOR 2: . . . said the Sea King, winding to a stop.

SEA KING: I could have danced for days. But a fine fellow you are, Sadko. I think I'll marry you to one of my daughters and keep you here forever.

SADKO: *(carefully)* Your Majesty, beneath the sea, your word is law. But this is not my home. I love my city of Novgorod.

SEA KING: Say no more about it! Now, behold your bride— the Princess Volkhova!

NARRATOR 1: The princess stepped forward. Her green eyes were sparkling, and a soft smile graced her lips.

VOLKHOVA: Dearest Sadko, at last we can be together. For years I have thrilled to the music you've played on the shore.

SADKO: *(in wonder)* Volkhova! You're as lovely as your river!

NARRATOR 2: But the Sea Queen leaned over and said softly,

SEA QUEEN: You are a good man, Sadko, so I will tell you the truth. If you but once kiss or embrace her, you can never return to your city again.

* * *

NARRATOR 1: That night, Sadko lay beside his bride on a bed of seaweed. He longed to hold her, but time after time, the Queen's words came back to him—

SEA QUEEN: *(voice only, offstage)* . . . never return to your city again . . .

NARRATOR 1: —and his arms stayed frozen at his sides.

VOLKHOVA: Dearest, why do you not embrace me?

SADKO: *(stammering a little)* It is the custom of my city. We never kiss or embrace on the first night.

VOLKHOVA: *(sadly)* Then I fear you never will.

NARRATOR 2: . . . and she turned away.

NARRATOR 1: When Sadko awoke the next morning, he felt sunlight on his face. He opened his eyes and saw beside him not the Princess Volkhova but the River Volkhov. And behind him rose the walls of Novgorod!

SADKO: My home.

NARRATOR 2: . . . said Sadko, and he wept—perhaps for joy at his return, perhaps for sadness at his loss, perhaps for both.

* * *

NARRATOR 1: The years were good to Sadko. With the money that remained to him, he bought a ship and goods enough to fill it. And so Sadko became a merchant, and in time, the richest man in Novgorod. What's more, he married a fine young woman and raised a family.

NARRATOR 2: Yet sometimes still on a quiet evening he would walk out of the city alone, sit on the bank, and send his tinkling music over the water. And sometimes too a lovely head would rise from the river to listen—

NARRATOR 1: or perhaps it was only moonlight on the Volkhov.

Author Online!

For more reader's theater, visit
Aaron Shepard's RT Page at

www.aaronshep.com/rt

About the Author

Aaron Shepard is the award-winning author of numerous picture books, as well as many stories in magazines like *Cricket* and Australia's *School Magazine*. Between 1986 and 1991, he was a professional actor in Chamber Readers, a nonprofit reader's theater troupe performing since 1975 in the schools of Humboldt County, California. During his five years with the troupe, he scripted and directed many of its performance pieces and led workshops for teachers and students. In 1986 and 1987, he also performed, scripted, and directed for the Radio Readers, on local public radio.

Aaron left professional reader's theater in 1991, when he moved from Humboldt County to pursue his career as a children's author. But in 1993 he published *Stories on Stage* (H. W. Wilson), considered by many the premier collection of reader's theater scripts.

Since 1994, Aaron has shared scripts on the Internet through his acclaimed series Reader's Theater Editions. First run as an email service, the series found its current home on the Web in 1996 as part of Aaron Shepard's RT Page (www.aaronshep.com/rt). This is today the Web's most popular reader's theater destination, with visits by thousands of teachers and librarians each week.

Aaron now lives in southern California.